THE ULTIMATE GUIDE TO ROMANTIC HOTELS

ITALY

2

LA DOLCE VITA STARTS HERE

L'Italia è molto bella. You can't argue with that – Italy is a richly beautiful country that seemingly has it all.

For a start, it's one vast end-to-end art emporium, heaving with classical paintings and sculptures, fabulous Renaissance buildings and medieval hilltop villages. No wonder Rome wasn't built in a day.

Italy also has great style – whether it's glamorous bars, fast cars or hot designer labels. It has terrific food. And its extraordinary mix of scenery – from snow-clad Alpine slopes and Tuscan hillsides to sun-drenched Sicilian beaches – puts it in a league of its own.

All this means that Italy has some fabulous places to stay. And Italy simply thrums with romance – it's tailor-made for a lovers' getaway. Where better then, to holiday with your *amore*?

Now you have decided on Italy for your romantic escape, the rest is easy. We have done all the homework, and you'll find details of 136 seductive places to stay between these covers. Some are shamelessly indulgent addresses where you may need to take a deep breath (or simply say what the hell) to splash out in style. Others are immensely affordable places of style and character. All are real tempters.

Whatever your kind of place – a 15th century Tuscan villa, a plush palazzo, designer B&B or chic chill-out address in the Aeolian Islands – you'll find it here. And while all are different, they share the essential qualities that make them tailor-made for romantic escapes: they are big on style, rich in ambience and individuality, and run by people passionate about great hospitality.

This is not an exhaustive guide to every inch of Italy. We have focused on the country's great city-break destinations as well as other easy-to-reach regions perfect for fans (like us) of Fly Cheap, Stay Chic travel. We show you where to stay when you get there.

Enjoy Italy. And just start turning these pages to find your idea of Hotel Heaven, Italian style.

MAIRIONA COTTER

EDITOR	Mairiona Cotter
CONTRIBUTORS	Mike North, Helen Pickles, Adele Evans
	Melissa Shales, Raz Murray
PRODUCTION	Zoë Munro, Katharina Hahn
DESIGN	Jenny White, Anabel Nunez
RESEARCH	Ben Etherton
PUBLICITY	Jemma Tabraham
ILLUSTRATIONS	Christine Coirault/frogillo.com
PHOTOGRAPHY	Zoë Munro, Roger Tabraham
WEBSITE	Alistair Ramsay
ADMIN	Kate Lee
HOTEL CONSULTANTS	Anna-Maria Baccanello, Giorgio Bonacini
	Maurice Moliver, Michael Yeo
PUBLISHER	Mairiona Cotter
PRINTING	Artes Gráficas Toledo
DISTRIBUTION	Portfolio Books: +44 (0) 20 8997 9000
Published in 2006	ISBN 0-9550944-0-2

RIVA PUBLISHING LTD
4 Ravey Street, London EC2A 4XX T +44 (0) 20 7739 1434 F +44 (0) 20 7739 1424
info@room4romance.com   www.room4romance.com
info@rivapublishing.com   www.rivapublishing.com
Copyright © 2006 Riva Publishing Ltd

CONTENTS

PHOTOGRAPHIC CREDITS

Photographs are reproduced with kind permission of the following hotels:
Page 55: Schwarz Adler Turm, Hotel Bellevue
Page 67: The Splendido, Stella Maris
Page 101: Corona d'Oro, La Fenice, Piana dei Castagni
Page 117: L'Andana, Borghetto di Chiena, La Suvera
Page 193: Villa Sanguigni, Il Palazzetto
Page 217: Ca' La Somara
Page 261: Il Palmento, Il Frantoio, Borgo San Marco

ABOUT ROOM FOR ROMANCE

This guide is the third – and biggest – edition of Room for Romance, the definitive series of guides to romantic escapes. They're designed to make the job of planning a romantic getaway as easy as falling into bed.

Following on the heels of our UK/Ireland and France editions, ROOM FOR ROMANCE ITALY is packed with details of places with style and individuality perfect for a lovers' getaway in Italy. Many come with canopied beds, roll-top baths for two, candlelit dining, indulgent spa treatments and other treats.

Our team have done the research. You just need to decide the kind of place you're after – somewhere to live it up, let your hair down, be pampered, be private, or simply be together.

We value your feedback on the places in this book, as well as details of your own discoveries in Italy. Do email us on info@room4romance.com.

If Room for Romance Italy whets your appetite for a great getaway, you need to read more about our other editions, Turn to page 315 for full details.

AWARD WINNERS
We make special awards each year to the hotels you tell us deserve special applause. Our winners to date are:

HOTEL OF THE YEAR – UK/IRELAND

2005	Prestonfield, Edinburgh
Runner up	Lewtrenchard Manor, Lewdown, Devon
2004	Amberley Castle, Nr. Arundel, Sussex
Runner up	Knockinaam Lodge, Portpatrick, Scotland
2003	Holbeck Ghyll, Windermere, Cumbria
Runner up	Combe House, Nr Honiton, Devon

HOTEL OF THE YEAR – FRANCE

2006	Château de Mazan, Mazan, Provence
Runner up	Hostellerie le Maréchal, Colmar, Alsace

SPECIAL ACCOLADES

The Witchery, Edinburgh (sexiest suites)
Isle of Eriska, Oban, Scotland (island idyll)
Nonsuch House, Devon (chic on a shoestring).

PRACTICALITIES

WHAT MAKES A ROOM FOR ROMANCE?

The properties featured in these pages embrace the best of Italy. They range from plush palazzi to chic and great-value B&Bs. They are here because they are ideally suited to romantic escapes, whether an impromptu weekend, a fly-drive holiday, a long-planned honey-moon, or a week in the sun.

The selection is ours alone – and we admit to being shamelessly subjective. Our team have chalked up several thousand miles in the quest to find the properties included here (and we naturally saw many that didn't make it into these pages), and we hope – though of course we cannot guarantee – that you'll love our final choices as much as we do.

All are appealing for different reasons – be it the location, the bedrooms, the cooking or the sheer originality and style. We hate conformity and blandness and have sought out properties with style, individuality and charisma perfect for indulgence. We don't look for stars and facilities so much as the vibe – the feel and philosophy of a place.

Hence you will find some Puglian beehive-shaped *trulli* hotels, and a few wonderful family-run country farmhouses as well as sumptuous palazzi worthy of a Roman emperor. Naturally you don't need to stay at a palace to have a great time, and we have tried to reflect all tastes and budgets in the diversity of addresses here.

We also look for places with indulgent and decadent bathrooms (those of you who responded to our recent readers' survey told us they are now your number one hotel treat), extravagant beds, atmospheric dining, exotically themed bedrooms, ultra-private suites and sensual spa treatments. We have flagged up these treats wherever they are available.

YOUR KIND OF PLACE

To make it easier to find the place that's right for you we have listed all properties at the back of the book under easy-to-follow categories.

So if you're after an intimate inn, foodie heaven, a spa hotel or a seriously splashy address for a special occasion, you'll find plenty of ideas. Turn to pages 312-314 for details.

EATING AND DRINKING

Food is one of the highlights of a trip to Italy (as they say, the Italians were eating with a knife and fork while the rest of us were still eating each other) whether it's a simple plate of pasta justa lika mamma used to make, or a six-course special. Cooking is still wonderfully regional in Italy, with ingredients based around the changing seasons.

Many Room for Romance properties offer excellent regional cooking prepared by the owners themselves using home-grown ingredients. City properties with-out their own restaurant will be happy to recommend great places to dine out.

OUR PAGE ENTRIES

As well as our giving you our overall view of the property in question, our reviews tell you which rooms and suites are worth booking for a special night.

If the swishy suites are way more than you want to pay, don't just turn up and hope for the best; speak to the hotel and see what they suggest. Many will throw down the red carpet for honey-mooners, while others will upgrade Room for Romance readers to the best available room (see page 11).

ROOM RATES, DINNER RATES

The rates quoted on our pages – eg 150-400 euros – are for a double room for two, with breakfast, unless otherwise stated. The lowest figure is the start rate in low season while the top one is the rate for the best category room or suite in the house. Since there is often a huge difference between the two, these figures should be used as a guideline only. You will need to check the exact rate for the room or suite of your choice.

Remember, too, that seasonal, midweek and low-season deals are common so check to see if there are any special promotional rates on offer. Visit our website www.room4romance.com for a selection of short break offers at different times of the year.

Dinner prices shown in our entries are for an average three-course dinner for two with a bottle of house wine, and again are intended for guidance only.

SPAS

No two hotel spas are the same, so if you're after the ultimate body-pampering experience do check just what is on offer at a hotel when you see our spa symbol. Some of the luxury spa properties featured here offer a fabulous range of treatments with all the trimmings. Others in more modest establishments are more likely to comprise a sauna, jacuzzi and fitness room, with perhaps an on-call beauty therapist of masseur. We suggest you check details when booking your stay rather than risk disappointment.

WWW.ROOM4ROMANCE.COM

Do visit our website from time to time to check out special short break offers and

other promotions at our hotels. You can also visit our Hotel of the Month, order copies of this and other editions online, see what the press say about us and enter competitions to win a stay at a Room for Romance hotel. You can also find out more about our Hotel of the Year winners – the properties you tell us are the cream of the crop.

SOME INFO ABOUT ITALY

When is a hotel not a hotel? Italians use many words other than Hotel or Villa to describe their property. To help you identify these at a glance, here are some examples you'll find in this book:

Masseria – an old fortified farmhouse, mainly in the south
Albergo – a hotel, often family run
Locanda – generally used to describe a restaurant, with or without rooms
Relais – an inn (as in French)
Ca' or Casa – a house (often in Veneto).

TELEPHONE CALLS

Don't be surprised to find different numbers of digits in Italian phone and fax numbers. All numbers start with an 0, whether calling from abroad or from within the country. This does not apply to mobile numbers, however, which never start with an 0. If you're in trouble, dial 113 for the emergency services.

DRIVING

Picking up a hire car at the airport is easy enough, though it's as well to remember that driving in Italy is not necessarily like at home. Cliff-edge roads with giddying drops in some parts are one feature that can take some getting used to, as can drivers riding a foot away from your back bumper. Watch the entry lanes on the *autostrada* – cars that should give way don't always. Towns are often full of *motorini* (scooters), an all-too-common hazard as they weave and dodge among traffic. Moral: take extra care.

Some Italian city names are different to English. Most are obvious, but Firenze (Florence) and Venezia (Venice) may keep you guessing.

MAPS

Our regional maps are not intended as driving aids – they are simply a visual signpost to show you the approximate location of each hotel relative to major roads or cities. You'll need a detailed road map to use the directions included on each page. Public transport and parking information is included for many city-centre hotels.

SHOP TILL YOU DROP

If you've had your fill of culture, you'll almost certainly need a retail fix – and Italy is the place to give your plastic a serious workout. Go to Venice for hand-blown glass (though beware the prices in some Murano and Burano showrooms), Florence for leather goods and Milan – Italy's fashion capital – for designer-label togs. Big spenders will be in retail heaven weaving their way down Rome's Via Condotti and Via Veneto, Florence's Via Tornabuoni and the chic boutiques of Bologna and Como. Food markets are great too, whether in the tiniest village or market town, and you'll want to go home stocked up with everything from jars of pesto to cantucci biscuits and Vin Santo.

ITALIAN TOURIST BOARD

For more travel information, a good starting point is the Italian tourist board. Contact details are:
UK: 020 7408 1254
italy@italiantouristboard.co.uk
www.italiantouristboard.co.uk

US: (212) 245 5618/4822
(312) 644 0996 (310) 820 1898
www.italiantourism.com

PARLA ITALIANO?

While most Room for Romance hoteliers speak English, do take a phrasebook and be ready to use it. We have listed some potentially useful phrases for your nights away on page 320.
Buon viaggio!

KEY TO SYMBOLS

Four-poster bed	Scenic location	Spa	Michelin star cuisine	Tennis
Golf	Weddings celebrated	Totally non-smoking	Restricted smoking	Swimming

If sporting facilities (eg tennis, golf) are not on site, the small figure in the right corner indicates the distance away in kilometres.

ROOM FOR ROMANCE EXTRAS

As a Room for Romance reader you will be welcomed with free extras at a number of the hotels in this book where you see the champagne glasses sign. It's thus easy to identify the places where you'll receive special surprises such as a bottle of champagne, welcome drinks, discounted rates or upgrades to a superior room.

To ensure you receive your Room for Romance extras it's important to state that you have read about the hotel in this guide when booking – and of course to have your copy when you arrive.

Please note that room upgrades are, by definition, subject to availability on the day and thus cannot be guaranteed.

Note: The offers detailed here – for instance room upgrades – are subject to availability on arrival. While the hotels named have elected to provide the extras and offers listed to individuals identifying themselves when booking as Room for Romance readers, the publishers cannot accept responsibility for hotels failing to honour any offer. (This may happen if, for instance, a hotel's ownership changes and the new proprietors fail to honour undertakings made by previous owners). Nor can the publishers assume responsibility for any loss, damage, disappointment, injury or inconvenience suffered as a result of a hotel's failure to honour any offer listed here. We recommend that readers confirm their booking with details of the Room for Romance extras detailed here, by email or letter.

ITALY – WHO FLIES WHERE ✈

Getting to Italy couldn't be easier – or cheaper– thanks to the growth in low-cost airline routes. Here are some of the options. For the full story, visit carriers' websites.

ALGHERO
London Stansted — Ryanair

ANCONA
London Stansted — Ryanair

BARI
London Stansted — R'air, BA

BOLOGNA
London Gatwick — BA
London Stanstes — Easyjet

BRINDISI
London Stansted — Ryanair

CATANIA
London Gatwick — BA

CAGLIARI
London Gatwick — BA
London Luton — Easyjet

FORLI (FOR BOLOGNA)
London Stansted — Ryanair

GENOA
London Stansted — R'air, BA

LAMEZIA
London Stansted — Ryanair

MILAN (BERGAMO)
Glasgow, Liverpool — Ryanair
Luton, Stansted — Ryanair
Newcastle — Ryanair

MILAN (LINATE)
London Gatwick — Easyjet

London Heathrow — Alitalia, BA, BMI

MILAN (MALPENSA)
Birmingham, Bristol — BA
London Gatwick — Easyjet
London Heathrow — A'lia, BA
Manchester — A'lia, BA

NAPLES
London Gatwick — BA
London Heathrow — BMI
London Stansted — Easyjet

OLBIA (SARDINIA)
London Gatwick — Easyjet

PALERMO
London Stansted — Ryanair

PARMA
London Stansted — Ryanair

PESCARA
London Stansted — Ryanair

PISA (FOR FLORENCE)
Bristol — Easyjet
Glasgow, Liverpool — Ryanair
London Gatwick — BA
London Stansted — Ryanair

ROME (CIAMPINO)
Bristol — Easyjet
Glasgow, Liverpool — Ryanair
London Gatwick — Easyjet
Luton, Stansted — Ryanair
Newcastle — Easyjet
East Midlands — Easyjet

ROME (FIUMICINO)
London Gatwick — BA
London Heathrow — A'lia, BA

TRIESTE
London Stansted — Ryanair

TREVISO (FOR VENICE)
Bristol — Easyjet
London Gatwick — BA, Easyjet
London Heathrow — BMI
Luton, Stansted — Ryanair
East Midlands — Easyjet

TURIN
London Gatwick — BA
London Luton — Easyjet
London Stansted — Ryanair

VENICE (MARCO POLO)
London Gatwick — Easyjet, BA
Manchester — BA

VERONA/BRESCIA
London Gatwick — BA
London Stansted — Ryanair

ALITALIA
alitalia.com

BMI BABY
bmibaby.com

BRITISH AIRWAYS
ba.com

EASYJET
easyjet.com

RYANAIR
ryanair.com

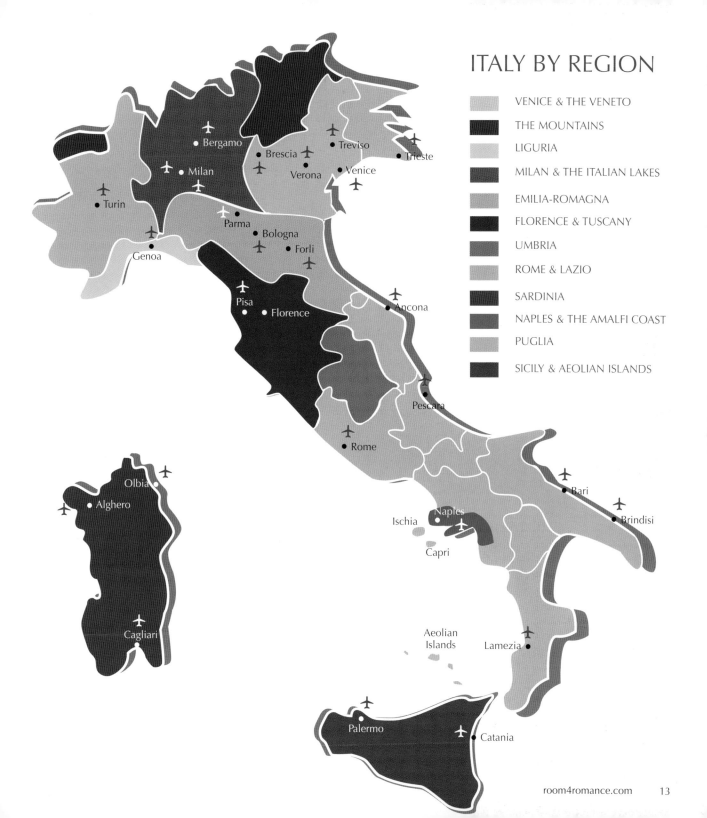

ITALY BY REGION

- VENICE & THE VENETO
- THE MOUNTAINS
- LIGURIA
- MILAN & THE ITALIAN LAKES
- EMILIA-ROMAGNA
- FLORENCE & TUSCANY
- UMBRIA
- ROME & LAZIO
- SARDINIA
- NAPLES & THE AMALFI COAST
- PUGLIA
- SICILY & AEOLIAN ISLANDS

Bergamo
Brescia
Treviso
Trieste
Milan
Verona
Venice
Turin
Parma
Bologna
Forli
Genoa
Pisa
Florence
Ancona
Pescara
Rome
Olbia
Alghero
Bari
Brindisi
Naples
Ischia
Capri
Cagliari
Aeolian
Islands
Lamezia
Palermo
Catania

VENICE &
THE VENETO

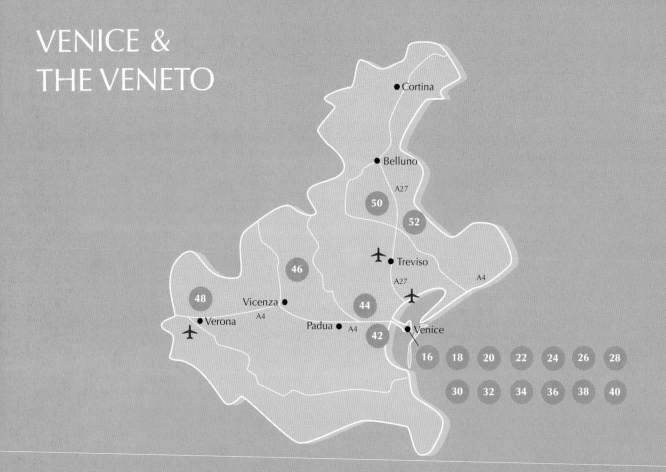

LOVE IT Venice is Europe's chocolate-box city of romance: an improbable jewel box of art, churches and palazzi wrapped in a filigree of canals. Behind it, the Veneto's great cities – Padua, Vicenza and Verona – ooze history. **When to go** Skip the crowds and visit Venice off-season. March can be sun-filled; November moody and misty; December and January wonderfully crisp and cold. Come in February for the famed ten-day Carnevale. **Don't miss** Must-sees like the Doge's Palace, the Guggenheim and the Basilica of San Marco. Zip along the Grand Canal in a vaporetto, wander the quiet streets of the Dorsoduro and visit the islands of the lagoon. There's a great open-air market at Santa Maria Formosa, and life doesn't get much smoochier than a gondola ride for two. Don't miss the Palladian villas of the Veneto and Verona's great opera festival. **Dine on** Great seafood, risotto cooked in Amarone wine (a Verona speciality), heavy bean soups and air-dried bresaola beef. Feeling brave? Try pastissada de caval (stewed horsemeat). **Drink up** A bellini – in the bar of at least one of the wonderful hotels detailed here.

CANALS, CAFES AND CARNEVALE

Pages 16-53

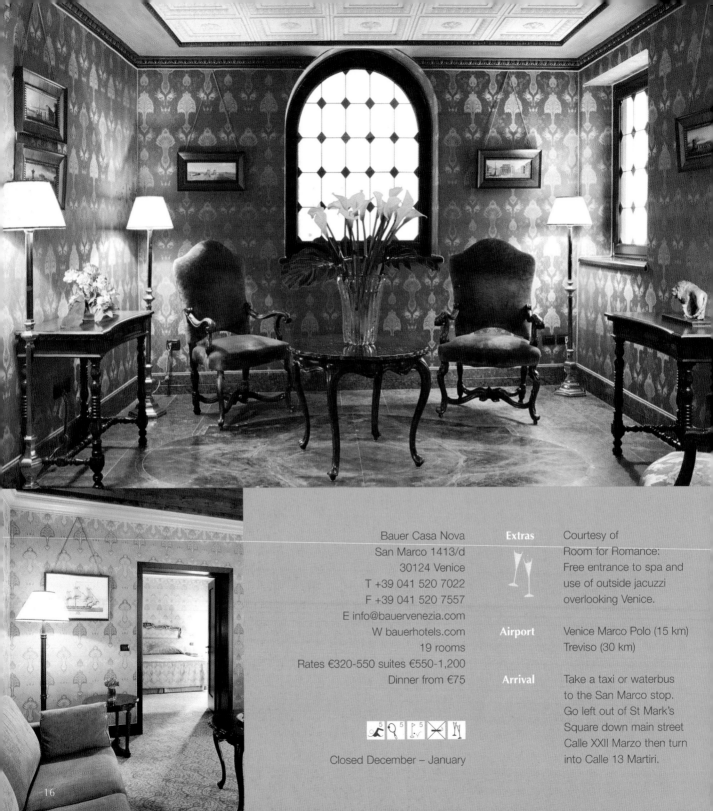

Bauer Casa Nova
San Marco 1413/d
30124 Venice
T +39 041 520 7022
F +39 041 520 7557
E info@bauervenezia.com
W bauerhotels.com
19 rooms
Rates €320-550 suites €550-1,200
Dinner from €75

Extras   Courtesy of
Room for Romance:
Free entrance to spa and
use of outside jacuzzi
overlooking Venice.

Airport   Venice Marco Polo (15 km)
Treviso (30 km)

Arrival   Take a taxi or waterbus
to the San Marco stop.
Go left out of St Mark's
Square down main street
Calle XXII Marzo then turn
into Calle 13 Martiri.

Closed December – January

Bauer Casa Nova

A newly opened offshoot of the famous Bauer Hotel, this restored 16th century mansion is an intimate hideaway only steps from Piazza San Marco. Traditional patterned walls in rich jewel colours, marble floors and bathrooms, heavy beamed ceilings and simple antiques create an enticing Venetian home away from home. With a kitchenette in all the suites and 24-hour room service from the hotel next door, you need never leave your room, although it would be heresy to miss the historic art treasures a stone's throw away. Inter-connecting doors allow guests to occupy one unit or an entire floor, while the penthouse has a Venetian wooden roof terrace or *altana* – tailor-made for midnight rambles or a glass of fizz before a night's partying. Guests have access to the five-star amenities of the Bauer, including round-the-clock concierge service, fitness centre, private docking and the gourmet De Pisis restaurant on the Grand Canal.

Love time   Casanova himself would have approved – he prowled these streets, perhaps he tested out these very rooms?

Love bites   Whip up a bowl of pasta in your suite, or head to the Bauer's lavishly grand restaurant next door.

Love it up   A loved-up weekend here is guaranteed to cure that sinking feeling. Awaiting exploration nearby are St Mark's Square and the Doge's Palace.

Bellissimo! ➤   Lap up the stylish home life of a Venetian aristocrat.

Ca Maria Adele
Dorsoduro 111
30123 Venice
T +39 041 520 3078
F +39 041 528 9013
E info@camariaadele.it
W camariaadele.it
Alessio & Nicola Campa
14 rooms
Rates €245-370

Open all year round

Extras   Courtesy of
Room for Romance:
A room upgrade
subject to availability.

Airport Venice Marco Polo (15 km)
Treviso (30 km)

Arrival Take a waterbus to Salute
stop. Walk down the right
of the Salute church and
the hotel entrance is on
your right. Or take a taxi
direct to the hotel's own
private landing stage.

Ca Maria Adele

This 16th century canalside palazzo in Dorsoduro has views to sigh for over the domes of Santa Maria della Salute. Glide into reception from your gondola to be embraced by charismatic luxury. The Venetian wooden raftered ceiling contrasts with a stripped-down minimalist look and African wood in the reception. White marble is reflected in majestic Murano glass chandeliers and all 14 light-suffused bedrooms blend simplicity with opulence. The mounds of inviting pillows and duvets are washed in a mountain laundry outside Venice to get that special Alpine freshness. Most have kingsize beds, waterfall showers and spacious walk-in wardrobes, leaving bedrooms free from untidy suitcases. Five 'concept' rooms invite you to immerse yourself in Venetian fantasy. The Doge's Room, dripping in rich red brocade, is for the master of the city – if your partner's feeling submissive. Sala dei Mori was inspired by the Moors, the Sala Orientale flaunts golds and blues, while Sala Noire in decadent black and chocolate recalls the old spice route.

Love time Surrender to Sala Noire's voluptuous colours and rich scents under a black Murano glass chandelier (cool off on the private roof terrace later).

Love bites Enjoy sundowners on the oriental terrace cocooned among silk cushions, lit by Moroccan lanterns. The setting for breakfast is just as sumptuous.

Love it up You're just five minutes from St Mark's and Santa Maria della Salute.

Bellissimo! Chic fusion of opulence and simplicity.

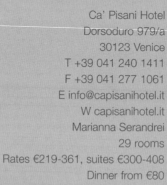

Ca' Pisani Hotel
Dorsoduro 979/a
30123 Venice
T +39 041 240 1411
F +39 041 277 1061
E info@capisanihotel.it
W capisanihotel.it
Marianna Serandrei
29 rooms
Rates €219-361, suites €300-408
Dinner from €80

Extras

Courtesy of
Room for Romance:
A complimentary chilled
bottle of prosecco in
your room.

Airport

Venice Marco Polo (15 km)
Treviso (30 km)

Arrival

Take a waterbus or taxi
to either the Accademia
or Zattere stops, then
walk down the Rio Terà
Foscarini.

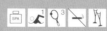

Open all year round

Ca' Pisani

Art Deco meets the 16th century here in a striking fusion of modernist taste and historic surrounds. This former palazzo has been transformed into a sleek temple to 1930s and '40s design – a cherub and frou-frou free zone for those who would sooner keep Venice's Baroque splendours outside the door. A flight of black marble steps leads to the lobby, glinting with marble and walnut wood. Walls are of Venetian stucco and the floors crafted with traditional terrazzo. Tones of terracotta, cream and chestnut brown dominate, leading the eye to original artworks and artefacts collected from all over Italy. Bedrooms are sleek and sexy – no chandeliers, heavy antiques or flamboyant decor here – and each is different. Eye-catchers include chunky black leather armchairs, retro-style anglepoise lamps and clean-limbed wood furniture. All have electric curtains – darkening the scene at the flick of a switch – while jacuzzi bathrooms are tiled in silver-speckled marble. Even room numbers are styled in etched wood in this striking one-time palazzo.

Love time   Some rooms have mezzanine lofts, while the penthouse has its own Turkish bath and a rooftop solarium.

Love bites   Dark red leather, steel lamps and well chosen art give La Rivista wine bar and restaurant a strikingly futuristic feel. There's great food, too.

Love it up   You're steps from the Grand Canal, Accademia Bridge and Guggenheim.

Bellissimo! ▶   Übercool address inside Venetian pink palace.

Hotel Casa Verardo
Campo San Filippo e Giacomo
Castello 4765, 30122 Venice
T +39 041 5286 138
F +39 041 5232 765
E info@casaverardo.it
W casaverardo.it
Francesco Mestre
20 rooms
Rates €90-360

Open all year round

Extras Courtesy of
Room for Romance:
A complimentary bottle
of prosecco and fresh
flowers in your room.

Airport Venice Marco Polo (10 km)
Treviso (30 km)

Arrival Take a taxi or waterbus to
the San Zaccaria stop,
then walk via Calle delle
Rasse, Campo San
Filippo e Giacomo and
Calle della Sagrestia.

Casa Verardo

In the mad maze of streets behind St Mark's Square, look for a pretty, wrought-iron balustraded bridge over a tiny canal. Quickly slip over and instantly enter a world of calm. Hard to believe this pool of tranquillity is but five minutes from the hurly-burly of central Venice, the grandeur of the Rialto and St Mark's Basilica. A typical tall and narrow 16th century Venetian palazzo, Casa Verardo is run with flair and genuine friendliness by the owners. Rooms are furnished with a refined, traditional elegance; terrazzo floors, gilded mirrors, carefully tended flowers, pretty chandeliers. Spread over three floors, bedrooms are high ceilinged, cool and calm oases, carefully and simply furnished perhaps with a carved bedhead or richly coloured drapes to add a special note. You feel like an old family friend rather than a hotel guest. After a busy day exploring, retreat here to the sunny rooftop terrace with its panoramic views of domes and bell-towers. Then slip downstairs to the terrace garden with its ancient well, terracotta pots and white cushioned wicker chairs and sip a prosecco amid the myriad twinkling tea-lights.

Love time   We loved the deluxe Room 305, tucked under the eaves, with open beams, parquet floor and private roof terrace.
Love bites   Typical Italian breakfasts are served on the tiny, sunny, flower-filled terrace.
Love it up   The owners offer free trips to the glass-making island of Murano.

Bellissimo! ❥   Gentle oasis in the city's heart.

Charming House DD724
Dorsoduro 724
30123 Venice
T +39 041 277 0262
F +39 041 296 0633
E info@dd724.com
W dd724.com
Chiara Bocchini
7 rooms
Rates €200-360

Open all year round

Extras　Courtesy of
Room for Romance:
A complimentary chilled
bottle of prosecco in your
room.

Airport　Venice Marco Polo (15 km)
Treviso (30 km)

Arrival　Take a waterbus or taxi to
the Accademia, turn left,
follow Guggenheim signs,
then continue onto Calle
della Chiesa. Entrance is
on left via an iron gate.

DD724

Everything is designed down to the last inch by architect Mauro Mazzolini in this quirkily named boutique B&B (actually its address – Dorsoduro 724 – trendily reduced to a stark code). Designer austerity reigns here, and if the city's banquet of brocade and Baroque is in danger of giving you overload, the crisp geometric lines, white walls and minimalist style of DD724 could be just the thing. Discreetly hidden by a heavy swirly wrought-iron door, it's tucked into an alleyway just off the Dorsoduro, minutes from the Guggenheim art museum and Accademia Bridge. Rooms overlook an ochre tapestry of Venetian backstreet windows and rooftops, while inside all is ultra-modern and über-chic. Hi-tech sound systems and flat-screen TVs, brown leather bedheads, specially woven bed throws, clever lighting, black mosaic-tiled bathrooms with chunky porcelain and satisfyingly large amounts of lotions and potions work together with style and panache. Owner Chiara Bocchini is passionate about design, as the strikingly displayed modern artworks and books on design testify. A perfect counterpoint to all that history.

Love time   Lots of room to play in the huge low beds with piles of plump pillows.
Love bites   Steaming coffee, sugary *cornetti* and four kinds of honey make breakfast worth getting up for. Afternoon tea is worth coming back for, too.
Love it up   Art fiends can head straight for the ground-breaking Guggenheim.

Bellissimo! ▶   Minimalist pied-à-terre with max in style.

The Cipriani
Giudecca 10
30133 Venice
T +39 041 520 7744
F +39 041 520 3930
E info@hotelcipriani.it
W hotelcipriani.com
Natale Rusconi
104 rooms, 58 suites
Rates €625-1,330
Dinner from €120

Open all year round

Extras

Courtesy of
Room for Romance:
A bottle of sparkling wine
and fresh flowers for
those staying in suites.

Airport

Venice Marco Polo (15 km)
Treviso (30 km)

Arrival

Free boat service to the
hotel every five minutes
24 hours a day from a
private landing stage at
Piazzetta San Marco
(beside St Mark's Square).

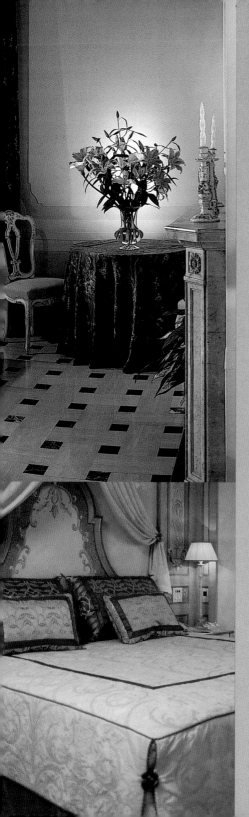

The Cipriani

Feel like a movie star. Arrive by private launch, walk through scented gardens, be greeted with dazzling smiles and infinite courtesy. And, for the time that you stay at this legendary hotel, you are one. Set on the secluded tip of Giudecca Island, across the lagoon from St Mark's Square, the Cipriani wraps you in luxury as though you were born to it. Yet its style is relaxed, unstuffy, unhurried. Five minutes from the bustle of this treasure-stuffed city, you're cocooned by manicured gardens, a vineyard, shady terraces, and an air of calm wellbeing. The style is understated, classical elegance but with enough wow factors to make you pinch yourself. Yes, it's all for real – kingsize beds, Fortuny fabrics, linen sheets, swish marble bathrooms, balconies and jacuzzis, and oodles of space. Book a suite in one of the 15th century palazzi and a personal butler takes care of everything. Swim in the Olympic sized outdoor pool, sip a bellini in the shade, be pampered in the Casanova Wellness Center, find a quiet corner in the gardens, gaze at one of the world's most shudderingly romantic skylines. Hey, it doesn't get much better than this.

Love time   For the max in ritzy decadence, book the Palladio or Dogaressa suites.
Love bites   Dine under the arched domes of the amber-mirrored Fortuny Restaurant or in the more hip, lagoon-side Cip's Club.
Love it up   Book an indulgent Babor massage, or zip off in a private launch.

Bellissimo!   Push the boat out on an island within an island.

Hotel Danieli
Castello 4196
30122 Venice
T +39 041 522 6480
F +39 041 520 0208
E danieli@luxurycollection.com
W luxurycollection.com/danieli
Claudio Staderini
222 rooms, 11 suites
Rates €299-924
Dinner from €235

Open all year round

Airport   Venice Marco Polo (15 km)
Treviso (30 km)

Arrival   From Marco Polo Airport:
take a water taxi direct to
the hotel's private landing
stage, or contact the
hotel direct to arrange
a private transfer.

The Danieli

This lavish gothic Venetian landmark – a former 14th century doge's palace – simply glows with Venice's golden past. Sitting in plum position by the lagoon, the Danieli has all the atmosphere of an ancient palazzo. Its palatial tone is set by a soaring, statement-making lobby clad in marble, complete with palm fronds, gothic arches and balustrades. There's also a sumptuous lounge area with glittering chandeliers and gold-leaf marble columns. The visual wow factor is not confined to the ground floor, either – head up to the rooftop bar and you can quaff a prosecco while watching Venetian sunsets to make your eyes mist over. Scores of stars have swept in from the hotel's private landing stage (Liz Taylor reputedly spent at least two of her honeymoons here) and vintage rooms invite you to sleep amid rich fabrics, frescoes, oil paintings and antiques. Like the grandest grande dame, the Danieli shows her age at times – and following in the footsteps of the doges naturally comes at a price. But for sheer old-time glamour this place is hard to beat.

Love time   Splash out on a room with a view in the old building for the full Danieli experience. If size matters, opt for the Victorian wing.

Love bites   Don't miss lunch in the rooftop restaurant. Be fussed over by white-gloved waiters while you make the most of the photo opportunities.

Love it up   You have Venice on a plate here; go and swim at a sister hotel on the Lido.

Bellissimo!   Vintage Venice landmark oozing star quality.

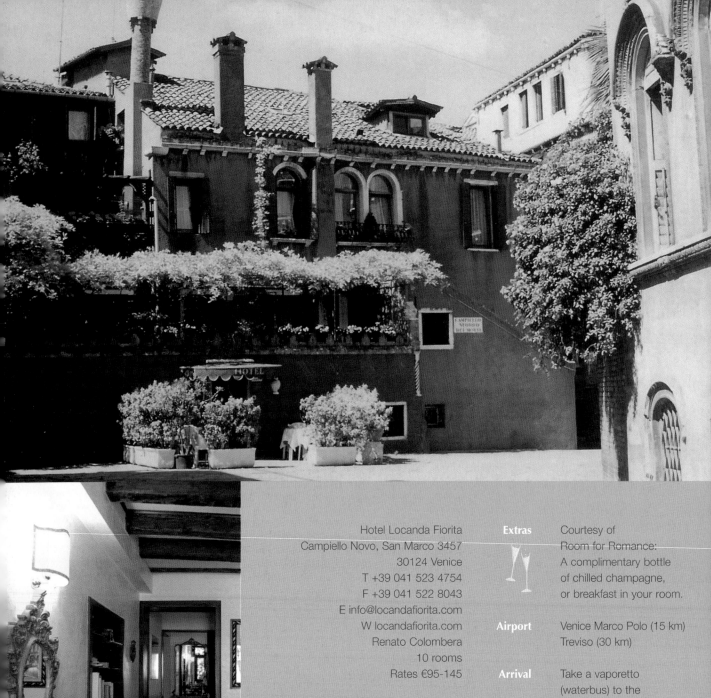

Hotel Locanda Fiorita
Campiello Novo, San Marco 3457
30124 Venice
T +39 041 523 4754
F +39 041 522 8043
E info@locandafiorita.com
W locandafiorita.com
Renato Colombera
10 rooms
Rates €95-145

Extras　Courtesy of
Room for Romance:
A complimentary bottle
of chilled champagne,
or breakfast in your room.

Airport　Venice Marco Polo (15 km)
Treviso (30 km)

Arrival　Take a vaporetto
(waterbus) to the
Sant'Angelo or San
Samuele stop. The hotel
itself is just near the
Santo Stefano church.

Open all year round

Locanda Fiorita

You can arrive almost at the door of this characterful Venetian villa by *vaporetto* – always fun in this city on the water. The other good news is that it's packed with affordable charm. Dating back to the 15th century, the pretty little pinky-brown palazzo is also close to the blockbuster sights of St Mark's and the Accademia galleries without being hemmed in by the tourist crowds. Greenery spreads across the walls and window boxes add colour in the summer months, when wrought-iron tables are set out facing the piazza (or *campiello*) in front; perfect for a lazy cappuccino breakfast in the sunshine. Renovation over the years has ensured that interiors retain their trademark wood beams, tiled floors and atmospheric charm while adding essential comforts. Simply furnished rooms (nab one in the main building rather than the annexe) mix modern furniture with Venetian style mirrors and country pieces. Not all are ensuite but two have little flower-decked terraces. The Fiorita may not make waves like Venice's showier places but its modest charms and good value certainly float our boat.

Love time   Breakfast al fresco under the leafy vine-clad pergola in warm weather.
Love bites   Vote yourselves into No 10: cupids on the walls, your own wisteria-clad terrace and views over the campiello in this pretty lovers' room.
Love it up   Staff can arrange trips to the glass-blowing islands of Murano and Burano.

Bellissimo! ▶   Tucked-away charmer that's still on top of things.

Hotel Flora
Calle Larga XXII Marzo
San Marco 2283/a
30124 Venice
T +39 041 520 5844
F +39 041 522 8217
E info@hotelflora.it
W hotelflora.it
Gioele Romanelli
44 rooms
Rates €140-290

Open all year round

Extras   Courtesy of
Room for Romance:
A complimentary chilled
bottle of prosecco in
your room.

Airport   Venice Marco Polo (15 km)
Treviso (30 km)

Arrival   Take a taxi or waterbus to
the San Marco stop. Go
left out of St Mark's
Square down Calle XXII
Marzo, then turn left down
Calle dei Bergamaschi.

Hotel Flora

This one-time 17th century palazzo, tucked down a little alleyway just minutes from Piazza San Marco, is an old Venetian favourite. Venice's history comes up to the very doorstep of the Flora, filled with 18th and 19th century Venetian pieces, and melting with charm. Rich covers are thrown over beds, wood floors are set off by rugs, sweeping curtains frame windows and intricate chandeliers provide focal points. A cosy sitting room is decorated in shades of red and an impressive marble staircase rises from the lobby. But the centrepiece of this old lovers' haunt is the jewel-like courtyard garden, with its climbing vines, ivy, laurel trees and profusion of summer flowers – just the place for aperitifs, breakfast or just scribbling postcards. Hands-on owners Ruggero and Gioele Romanelli and their nothing's-too-much-trouble staff keep things ticking like clockwork and the guestbook speaks volumes: devotees taken with the Flora's charm and hospitality clearly return here year after year. We'll be back, too.

Love time   Bedrooms vary, with the nicest overlooking the courtyard. Try and bag a corner room with all-round views.

Love bites   The courtyard is just the place for a laid-back breakfast or a nightcap.

Love it up   Palazzo Contarini Fasan, home of Othello's Desdemona, is next door. Piazza San Marco and the Grand Canal are just minutes away.

Bellissimo! ▶   Venetian gem in secluded corner.

Hotel Londra Palace
Riva degli Schiavoni 4171
30122 Venice
T +39 041 520 0533
F +39 041 522 5032
E info@hotelondra.it
W hotelondra.it
Mauro Zanotti
53 rooms
Rates €275-585, junior suites €485-790
Dinner from €150

Open all year round

Extras   Courtesy of
Room for Romance:
A complimentary bottle
of prosecco and a 15%
discount in the hotel's
restaurant.

Airport   Venice Marco Polo (15 km)
Treviso (30 km)

Arrival   Take a waterbus to the
San Zaccaria stop, then
turn right along the lagoon
for 10m. You can also take
a taxi directly to the hotel.

Londra Palace

With 100 windows overlooking the Venetian lagoon and the island of San Giorgio, these are rooms with a view to shout about. The reflection of this graceful neo-classical hotel clad in white Istrian marble glistens in the waters of the lagoon. Inside it's all space and airiness. Venetian glass, inlaid mosaic floors, 19th century antiques, pale silk-lined walls and chairs, thickest pile Aubusson carpets and occasional splashes of red create striking interiors. Diaphanous curtains dress the windows, mirroring that luminous Venetian light – a light that inspired Peter Tchaikovsky, no less, to compose his fourth symphony here. (Note to music fans: Room 106 has memorabilia of the great man). The feeling of unobtrusive luxury extends to lavish and individually designed bedrooms, with pink marble bathrooms (the best having brass and porcelain fittings), silk and brocade furnishings and period objets d'art. We climbed up to the roof terrace by the spiral staircase, where the Campanile and La Serenissima are spread before you. If you're not out of breath, this is a place to pop the question – or at least a cork or two.

Love time	We'd have a tryst in the suite in the eaves with a jacuzzi next to the skylight.
Love bites	Eight different kinds of bread are baked here daily. The excellent Do Leoni restaurant's wicked chocolates and icecream are hand-made too.
Love it up	You're just a sigh away from that famous bridge and Piazza San Marco.

Bellissimo! ▶ Lavish rooms and matchless views in Venice's heart.

Metropole Hotel
Riva degli Schiavoni 4149
30122 Venice
T +39 041 520 5044
F + 39 041 522 3679
E venice@hotelmetropole.com
W hotelmetropole.com
Eugenio Rigo
70 rooms
Rates €200-650, suites €400-1,000
Dinner from €65

Open all year round

Extras

Airport

Arrival

Courtesy of
Room for Romance:
'Romantic Corner'
bath treat with orchids,
candles, bath salts
and special perfume.

Venice Marco Polo (15 km)
Treviso (30 km)

Take a waterbus to San
Zaccaria stop. Turn right
and walk along the
lagoon for 200m to
the hotel.

The Metropole

This cult boutique hotel overlooks the Venetian lagoon a mere gondola glide from St Mark's Square. A kissing chair in the foyer is just a taste of the romance-laden interiors within. Rich dark wood, glittering chandeliers, gilded mirrors, bronze cherubs, precious velvets, sensual silks, original antiques and collections of rare artefacts grace every nook. Built on the site of the church where Vivaldi once composed and performed, you can still walk in the great composer's footsteps on the old stone spiral staircase. Sip an *aperitivo* in the Salone degli Specchi, ensconced in plush red velvet with views of the Grand Canal glinting in antique mirrors and Murano glass. And rub shoulders with a galaxy of glitterati who have made the Met restaurant their home from home, where gifted young chef Corrado Fasolato cooks up a creative storm with his innovative take on the traditional. We found the perfumed garden set around a fountain-splashed courtyard quite magical by candlelight. This is a place for all the senses – the inspiration for Vivaldi's Four Seasons.

Love time   Bedrooms come with crisp linen, down pillows, soft silks, Etro toiletries and incense. The Angels' suite is a fantasy of trompe l'oeil frescoes.

Love bites   Be daring: try sturgeon tartare or lobster ravioli with wasabi sauce. Nibble on pastries during the famous candlelit, incense-perfumed afternoon tea.

Love it up   Bliss out amid the Bar Zodiaco's antique cushions, silks, and incense.

Bellissimo!   Hip, chic and boutique. You want more?

Novecento
Calle del Dose 2684
Campo San Maurizio, 30124 Venice
T +39 041 241 3765
F +39 041 521 2145
E info@novecento.biz
W novecento.biz
Gioele Romanelli
9 rooms
Rates €140-260

Open all year round

Extras Courtesy of
Room for Romance:
A complimentary chilled
bottle of prosecco
in your room.

Airport Venice Marco Polo (15 km)
Treviso (30 km)

Arrival Take a taxi or waterbus
to Santa Maria de Giglio.
Turn left at Campo Maria
del Giglio into Campo San
Maurizio, then left again
into Calle del Dose.

Novecento

If Venice oozes a peerlessly evocative atmosphere then this little boutique townhouse gilds the lily. Step across the threshold and its charms grab you immediately. The hotel's interior is inspired by the famous fin-de-siècle painter and fashionista Mariano Fortuny, whose inimitable style is overlaid on an eclectic melange of oriental furnishings. There's something very seductive about this sort of aesthetic. We adored the lush signature wallpapers and fabrics, polished wood floors, log fires and curiosities. There are only nine bedrooms, and each is individually styled. In one there's a nod to the mysterious East; another exudes the clubbyness of an Edwardian gentleman traveller's life; one is distinctly Moorish and recreates your own little Kasbah; while another with an iron four-poster, raw silk hangings and rafters above could easily take your fancy. (Mod cons aren't overlooked in all this either). Owners the Romanellis see to it that guests are swept up in the magic of the place. Just check the visitor's book to see the spell it casts.

Love time We took the Thai route… and slunk into a characterfully low wooden bed with fresh white linens, lit some candles and marvelled at our Venetian view.
Love bites Fine weather sees the little courtyard's tables laden with scrumptious breakfasts, while the Moroccan-style sitting room offers day-long drinks.
Love it up Regular art and sculpture exhibitions are held on site – an added buzz.

Bellissimo! 🍷 Glittering little gem pinned to the bustle of Venice.

San Clemente Palace Hotel & Resort
Isola di San Clemente
30124 Venice
T +39 041 244 5001
F +39 041 244 5800
E sanclemente@thi.it
W sanclemente.thi.it
Michele Zanconato
118 rooms, 82 suites
Rates €286-3,080
Dinner from €70

Open all year round

Extras

Courtesy of
Room for Romance:
A complimentary chilled
bottle of prosecco in your
room.

Airport

Venice Marco Polo (17 km)
Treviso (30 km)

Arrival

There's a free shuttle boat
service to and from the
hotel every 20 minutes 24
hours a day from a private
landing stage at Piazzetta
San Marco.

San Clemente Palace

If nothing but your own private island will do, then it has to be the San Clemente Palace. Leave the crowds behind, hop aboard the hotel's private launch and ride across the Venice lagoon to this five-star resort in acres of lush parkland. Contemporary in style yet with origins dating back to the 12th century – the medieval church still remains – it combines luxe and lavish amenities with views of Venice set against a backdrop of the Dolomites. Marble hallways lined with cases of luxury goods and portraits of the doges lead to spacious rooms built for every comfort, with high Venetian ceilings, crisp white linen, elegant furnishings and expensive fabrics. Marble bathrooms – some with sweeping views – come with twin basins, deep tubs and a generous stock of toiletries. Sumptuous suites bear the names of the giants in Venice's history: Canaletto, Tintoretto and Titian. Four restaurants cater for every taste. Outside, groomed lawns lead down to the lagoon and a large secluded pool. You might even do some star-spotting: big names like Robert De Niro, the Oasis brothers and Keira Knightley come here to escape the paparazzi.

Love time   Let go amid heaps of baby-soft pillows piled on shamelessly over-sized beds.
Love bites   Sip a cocktail at the American bar before an indulgent dinner in the Ca dei Frati restaurant, whose lagoon views are matched by top-notch cuisine.
Love it up   See Venice's big sights, then pamper body and soul at the beauty club.

Bellissimo!   Plush palazzo on peaceful Venetian isle.

Villa Margherita
Via Nazionale 416
30030 Mira Porte, Venice
T +39 041 426 5800
F +39 041 426 5838
E info@villa-margherita.com
W villa-margherita.com
The Dal Corso family
19 rooms
Rates €198-246
Dinner from €150

Open all year round

Extras Courtesy of
Room for Romance:
Upgrade (if in deluxe
room or junior suite).
Prosecco, basket of fruit,
plus room service.

Airport Venice Marco Polo (15 km)
Treviso (25 km)

Arrival From Venice: take A4 to
Dolo–Mirano exit. At Dolo
town centre go left for
Venice. Hotel signed after
4 km in Mira Porte.

Villa Margherita

Centuries back when Venetian patricians tired of life in the city they sought a touch of R&R in Palladian villas built along the River Brenta. A taste of that sumptuous lifestyle lives on at Villa Margherita. The original 16th century building lies in peaceful parkland at the end of an imposing avenue lined with towering lime trees interspersed with statues. The interior is equally eye-catching. Parlour and drawing room glory under murals of nymphs at their toilette while allegorical frescoes crown ceilings. Period furniture, Persian rugs and contemporary pieces jostle with flair; logs burn in marble fireplaces and the glow from ornate lamps reflects in gold-leaf mirrors. Suites continue the feeling of richesse. The breakfast room is generously roomy with finely dressed tables and a terrace for good weather. Ristorante Margherita – a neighbourhood favourite – looks exquisite with crystal, floral arrangements, thick primrose napery and bone china. Chef Remigio Dal Corso creates exacting fish dishes in Venetian style accompanied by regional grand-crus. This Margherita could easily be summed up as a cocktail of top-notch ingredients.

Love time   Traditional elegance rules. Rooms have comfortable antiques, large beds with rich covers, draped French windows and – in many – a terrace.

Love bites   Don't miss classic Venetian seafood in the hotel's stand-alone restaurant.

Love it up   Walk the parkland, or get waterborne in Venice just 10 km away.

Bellissimo! ▶   Veneto country classic with va-va-voom.

Villa Rizzi Albarea
Via Albarea 53
30030 Pianiga di Venezia
T +39 041 510 0933
F +39 041 513 2562
E info@villa-albarea.com
W villa-albarea.com
Aida and Pierluigi Rizzi
7 rooms, 1 suite
Rates €200-280 (min 2 night stay)

Open all year round

Extras Courtesy of
Room for Romance:
A bottle of Italian wine and
fresh roses in your room.

Airport Venice Marco Polo (16 km)
Treviso (30 km)

Arrival From Milan-Venice A4:
take Casello di Dolo exit
after Padua. Go straight
over two sets of lights
then follow signs for
Albarea. Villa Rizzi is
then signposted.

44

Villa Rizzi Albarea

Few addresses can boast their own private chapel, but this place was originally built 1,000 years ago as a monastery. You needn't be religious to marvel at its beauty, with a ceiling by Tiepolo and paintings from the Tintoretto school. Nor does the handsomely colonnaded villa (the most ancient on the Brenta Riviera) stint on beauty elsewhere. Take its two acre park, complete with sylvan woodland studded with statues, rose bushes and a little bridge-crossed lake where herons dive and swans glide (bird-watch unseen from the wisteria-clad gazebo and tower). The interior continues the visual aesthetic: hall, library, drawing and music rooms groan with heavily decorated ceilings and chandeliers, while walls are dressed in fine tapestries and murals set off by good antiques. In addition there's a pool sheltered by clipped hedges and a spa with a menu of beauty treatments (why not look the part if all around you does?). The Albarea's hospitality is extended by aristocratic owners Pierluigi and Aida Rizzi, who have spent 30 years refurbishing it within Belle Arti guidelines. Definitely a case of 'putting on the Rizzi' for their guests.

Love time   Lavishly decorated bedrooms have canopied beds with lace-trimmed linens.
Love bites   Tables glow by candlelight at night. Note the family-crested porcelain.
Love it up   You're 'twixt Padua and Venice here: ideal for country walks, golf and riding, or day trips to the glass-blowing islands of Burano and Murano.

Bellissimo! Ancient Venetian villa enveloped by elegance.

Relais Ca' Masieri
Via Masieri
36070 Trissino
T +39 044 549 0122
F +39 044 549 0455
E info@camasieri.com
W camasieri.com
Angelo Vassena
12 rooms
Rates €100-160
Dinner from €80

Extras
Courtesy of
Room for Romance:
A complimentary bottle
of sparkling wine in
your room.

Airport
Treviso (70 km)
Venice Marco Polo (75 km)

Arrival
From the Milan-Venice
A4: take the Montecchio
exit and follow signs for
Trissino, then Masieri.

Open all year round

46

Ca' Masieri

Ca' Masieri is reckoned to be the business when it comes to creatively interpreted regional cuisine, prepared according to the seasons. It's a stylish restaurant with 18th century frescoes, well-dressed tables and immaculately attired waiters. Stuffy then? Not a bit. Our beautifully-judged meal prepared by award-winning chef Enrico Bassani included fresh ravioli with a duck farci and caramelised orange butter. The next evening saw us dining outside under a portico nibbling on fried oysters with risotto and black truffles (heaven) followed by pineapple carpaccio marinaded in passion fruit juice. A smooth Durello – one from a notable wine list – washed things down nicely. Attention to our plates didn't exclude noticing the other pleasing features of this attractively converted 18th century farmstead with its vista of hills and evocative countryside. The decor mixes simple modern pieces with homey period features. A shuttered carriage-house has been comfortably given over to wood-beamed bedrooms, while at night the courtyard and pool are romantically floodlit. All in all, we'd say Ca' Masieri is quite a dish.

Love time	Light-filled rooms have a contemporary feel, often with hillside views.
Love bites	There's top-notch cooking in elegant surrounds: tuck into caviar with carrot salsa, pigeon casserole, aromatic herb sorbets, great cheeses.
Love it up	You're close to ancient Vicenza, Padua and Verona, and rugged country.

Bellissimo! Foodie's paradise in the Veneto.

Relais La Magioca
Via Moron 3
37024 San Vito di Negrar
T +39 045 600 0167
F +39 045 600 0840
E info@magioca.it
W magioca.it
Matteo Merighe
6 rooms
Rates €190-250

Open all year round

Extras

Courtesy of
Room for Romance:
A selection of home-made
chocolates in your room.

Airport

Verona (20 km)

Arrival

From Verona: take the
A22, exit at Verona Nord
and take SS12 for
Valpolicella and Negrar.
At Santa Maria lights turn
left, then left again after
1 km towards Moron.

La Magioca

Pluck fresh fruit from the orchard, wander through the olive grove, doze in the hammock. Nothing to disturb the view but vineyards and the distant skyline of Verona. Hidden in the depths of Valpolicella country, this sprawling stone farmhouse is as deeply calming as it is solidly built. Its handsome facade – green shuttered windows, creeper covered walls and shady terrace – does not disappoint once you step inside. Antiques, deep sofas and rich rugs on polished floors are generously spread around. Help yourself to drinks in the large and airy sitting room where soft music floats in the background. The six bedrooms, in warm tones of yellow, ochre and rust, are elegantly furnished giving a sense of space and richness. Bold paintings, Tuscany-made linen and flowers from the garden add luxurious and personal touches. While Verona, Valpolicella country and Lake Garda are on your doorstep, you might find it hard to tear yourself away from the garden with its sunny and shady spots, ancient seats and pretty Romanesque 13th century church.

Love time   The suite has the four-poster – but the Room of the Mosaics, with its raftered ceiling and mosaic-walled bathroom, is pretty tempting.
Love bites   Breakfast on delicious bread and plum cake, fresh fruit and sizzling coffee.
Love it up   Check out the Valpolicella vineyards, book opera tickets (in season) in Verona, sail on Lake Garda or soak in the garden's outdoor hot tub.

Bellissimo!   Relaxed country house living, Veneto style.

Villa Abbazia
Piazza IV Novembre 3
31051 Follina
T +39 043 897 1277
F +39 043 897 0001
E info@hotelabbazia.it
W hotelabbazia.it
Giovanni Zanon
12 rooms, 6 suites
Rates €180-450
Dinner from €80

Closed January

Extras

Courtesy of
Room for Romance:
Special price for airport
shuttle (min stay 3 nights);
green fees.

Airport

Treviso (48 km)
Venice Marco Polo (72 km)

Arrival

From Venice: Take the A4
north, then A27 towards
Belluno. Exit at Conegliano
and follow signs to Follina
and Abbazia Santa Maria
XII Siecle.

Villa Abbazia

Venetian gentry used to journey into the Treviso region years back to escape the urban blues. Green, tranquil and set against the foothills of the Alps, their escape still holds good. Bang opposite a 13th century abbey, Villa Abbazia sits in pretty Follina. Two impressive buildings – one, a 17th century villa, retains many old architectural details – while the other, clad in ivy, was added in Victorian times. Linking them is a pretty courtyard garden with magnolia trees and blooms bursting from pots. There's a come-hither terrace (perfecto for al fresco), a café and little wine bar. Country-house style decoration is pulled off with taste and flair, while the Zanon family's warmth and welcome gives it all the appeal of a private home. Softly lit with trompe l'oeil murals, La Corte restaurant offers Veneto classics alongside local Treviso seductions. Breakfasts are something else too: good food and a great start-the-day setting under the magnolia tree has even landed the hotel a Best in Italy award. The uphill, down dale scenery hereabouts is popular with movie makers and you can see why; evocative old towns, Palladian villas galore, vineyards producing some of Italy's finest bubbles. The Abbazia sparkles in equal measure.

Love time   Suites with a jacuzzi, private terrace and garden views should do the trick.
Love bites   Elegant La Corte delivers Venetian cuisine with an imaginative twist.
Love it up   Bike, swim or ride; learn to cook; take vineyard trips or day trips into Venice.

Bellissimo! ➤   Fizzes stylishly – break open the prosecco!

Hotel Villa Giustinian
Via Giustiniani 11
31019 Portobuffolè, Treviso
T +39 042 285 0244
F +39 042 285 0260
E info@villagiustinian.it
W villagiustinian.it
Nathalie Berto
35 rooms, 8 suites
Rates €138-150, suites €300-365
Dinner from €72

Closed 3-23 January

Extras   Courtesy of
Room for Romance:
A room with a view of the
park and a complimentary
bottle of prosecco.

Airport   Treviso (38 km)
Venice Marco Polo (45 km)

Arrival   From Treviso: follow
signs for Oderzo then
Pordenone. The hotel is
on the main road 8 km
from Oderzo.

Villa Giustinian

If you love making grand entrances, this is the place to be. Sweep up the drive and into the ballroom-sized entrance hall of this blindingly white 17th century villa and prepare to be smitten. Every surface shimmers and glows – from the Murano glass chandeliers and gleaming white staircase to the delicately frescoed walls, gilded mirrors and polished grand piano. This was how Venetian noble families lived and, boy, are you going to do the same. Painstaking effort has been made to preserve the villa's original flamboyant style, subtly mixed with modern comforts. Bedrooms are grand with rich fabrics, elaborate stucco work, hand-painted and gold-inlaid furniture, thick carpets and burnished wood floors. Should you drag yourself away from their sybaritic comforts, there's a vast Italian style park at your disposal. Its immaculate lawns are studded with half-draped statues, a pool and shady private corners. The staff here dispense true Venetian hospitality.

Love time   Choose between rooms in the former stables, with their whitewashed walls and beams, and the villa's more formal grand Baroque suites.

Love bites   Eat Veneto specialities and browse a list of over 500 cellared wines. In summer, dine under white awnings in the softly-lit garden.

Love it up   Be whisked away to Venice in a private limo, discover the walled town of Treviso or explore the Veneto's Palladian villas.

Bellissimo!   Sumptuous style, gracious living in the Veneto.

THE MOUNTAINS

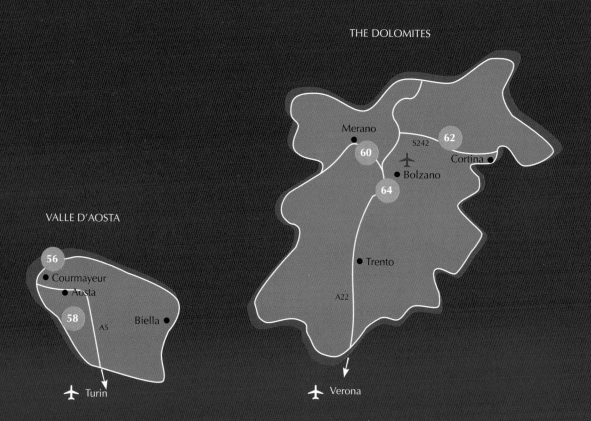

THE DOLOMITES

Merano
S242
62
60
Cortina
Bolzano
64
Trento
A22

VALLE D'AOSTA

56
Courmayeur
Aosta
58
Biella
A5

Turin

Verona

LOVE IT There are definite shades of Austria in the region studded with jagged Dolomite peaks north of Verona. Like Valle d'Aosta, tucked into the north-west corner of Italy, this is winter ski country as well as great walking terrain. **When to go** Early summer for walking and fabulous mountain flowers; winter for a snow blanket. **Don't miss** The great outdoors. Roam through pine-clad slopes and pastureland, picnic in the mountains, spot eagles and ibex, scale (or ski) the peaks. Courmayeur boasts Europe's highest golf course, and summer brings rafting and mountain biking. The cable car ride to the Aiguille du Midi – highest point of Mont Blanc – is a stunner, while Valle d'Aosta's Gran Paradiso national park is awesome. **Dine on** Hearty mountain fare with a Germanic twist: dumplings and Speck (smoked ham), venison stew made with a dash of grappa, or costoletta alla Valdostana – veal dipped in breadcrumbs, wrapped in ham and local Fontina cheese. **Drink up** Wines from the highest vineyards in Europe. Standout reds include Donnas and Chambave Rosso and the full-bodied Nus Rosso.

SNOW, SCENERY & SPA PAMPERING

Pages 56-65

Auberge de la Maison
Entrèves
11013 Courmayeur, Valle d'Aosta
T +39 0165 869 811
F +39 0165 869 759
E info@aubergemaison.it
W aubergemaison.it
Leo Garin
54 rooms
Rates €120-190
Dinner from €65

Closed May

Extras

Courtesy of
Room for Romance:
Free entry for two to the
sauna and Turkish bath.

Airport

Geneva (98 km)
Turin (110 km)

Arrival

From Turin: take A4, then
A5 towards Aosta. Exit at
Courmayeur onto the E25
and follow signs to Traforo
del Monte Bianco and the
hotel itself.

Auberge de la Maison

Faithful to its name, this chalet is a home from home in a winter wonderland. Gazing straight out at Mont Blanc (Monte Bianco), it's at the foot of Europe's loftiest mountain. The charming wood and stone auberge is set in picture-pretty Entrèves in the Courmayeur valley. Built in 1996, the chalet blends perfectly into this rustic Alpine village that oozes charm. The welcoming lobby gleams with natural wood, but the highlight is the old chalet, faithfully recreated from antique, wild wood. Big puffy sofas and a blazing fire invite you to curl up and savour fabulous views of the jagged Dente del Gigante. From the 33 windows there are as many different views over spectacular Alpine peaks and valleys. Each bedroom is individually designed, with a large balcony, antiques and natural wood cosiness. After a hard day at play – on or off the piste – slope off into the hotel's *benessere* centre to discover the pleasure of wellbeing in the hammam, sauna and solarium. Snuggle up over a cocktail as night falls and the snow glints like diamonds.

Love time	Top-floor suites have intimate low roofs and deep tubs – perfect for amorous Snow Whites. Suite 307 even has an open fire to melt in front of.
Love bites	Try a *fondita* of local cheeses and leave room for the wicked puddings.
Love it up	Join the evening *passeggiata* on Via Roma when everyone struts and preens to see and be seen. Chic Courmayeur is stuffed with great bars and shops.

Bellissimo!   Intimate, snow-struck mountain chill-out.

Hotel Bellevue
Rue Grand Paradis 22
11012 Cogne, Valle d'Aosta
T +39 0165 74825
F +39 0165 749 192
E bellevue@relaischateaux.com
W hotelbellevue.it
Jeantet Roullet
38 rooms
Rates €160-330
Dinner from €60

Airport   Turin (128 km)

Arrival   From Turin: take the A5 to Aosta, go through town and turn left onto the R47, following signs to Cogne.

Closed mid October – November

Hotel Bellevue

Perched at 1,500 metres on the edge of Gran Paradiso National Park, you could get high here on the air alone. Glowing with warm woods, roaring fires and handsome antiques, this hotel is like a luxurious mountain chalet. Blink awake to crystal views of snow-capped Mont Blanc and Gran Paradiso and the glitter of snow. Traditional hand-crafted furniture, richly coloured fabrics and rustic pieces are set against polished wood floors, raftered ceilings and massive fireplaces. Bedrooms are like the cosiest and rosiest of log cabins. Walls are warmly-coloured or wood-panelled, ceilings beamed, floorboards scattered with rugs. There are bright red and white checked fabrics, shelves of books, displays of local craftwork and – in most – heart-thumping mountain views. After an invigorating day out, return to afternoon tea and home-made cakes by a roaring fire. Or indulge all the senses in the award winning Happy Valley – La Valheureusa – spa. Frolic among the water cascades, turn up the heat in the sauna, submit to a rasul mud clay bath, soak in milk and honey or be blissfully revived with a bio-energetic massage.

Love time   Get cosy in a suite: log fire, canopied bed, and a private sauna or jacuzzi.
Love bites   Dine in the Michelin starred restaurant, mountain inn or buzzing brasserie.
Love it up   Bliss out in the spa's King Victor Bath; a bronze bathtub for two filled with mountain spring water and spiced local wine, with champagne on the side.

Bellissimo!   Spa time in the mountains.

Castel Rundegg Hotel & Beauty Farm
Schennastrasse 2
39012 Merano
T +39 0473 234 100
F +39 0473 237 200
E info@rundegg.com
W rundegg.com
Peter Castelforte
30 Rooms
Rates €200-300
Dinner from €120

Open all year round

Extras

Courtesy of
Room for Romance:
A room upgrade and
bottle of sparkling wine
(min two night stay).

Airport Bolzano (27 km)

Arrival From Brescia: take A4
towards Verona, then A22
for Bolzano/Bozen. Turn
onto SS38 for Merano;
exit Merano 2000/Scena
and follow yellow signs
for hotel.

Castel Rundegg

If you think you've strayed into Austria, you're almost right. This Tyrolean castle, with its towers and prettily shuttered windows, has a distinctly Alpine air. Surrounded by lush, semi-tropical gardens and gentle promenades, there's more than a slight feeling that you've wandered onto a film set – and a luxury one at that. Grand stone pillars, vaulted and decorated ceilings, polished terracotta floors and majestic windows remain from its medieval past. Darkly polished antiques, glittering chandeliers, rich fabrics and deep sofas maintain the princely style, while vast bedrooms, many with balconies or private gardens, have a country house elegance without going over the top. This old-world Alpine address is also a new-world spa and beauty farm with an array of therapies and treatments designed to send you home glowing with good health. You can go the whole hog with a full-on, week-long detox, bio-energetic and rejuvenating programme or simply indulge in a menu of pampering massages, facials, hay baths and aromatherapy… drifting afterwards from sauna to swimming pool to sun terrace.

Love time   The attic rooms make cosy love nests, while the Tower has stunning views.
Love bites   Go for the full gastronomic works or a detox special? Decisions, eh…
Love it up   Book an anti-stress massage, a Cleopatra bath or a body peel and feel a
                  new person. Limber up with some yoga, physio or aquarobics.

Bellissimo!   Spa-spangled Tyrolean castle.

Hotel & Spa Rosa Alpina
Strada Micura de Rü 20
39030 San Cassiano in Badia
T +39 0471 849 500
F +39 0471 849 377
E info@rosalpina.it
W rosalpina.it
Hugo Pizzinini
54 rooms and suites
Rates €250-625
Dinner from €152

Closed April-May and Oct-Nov

Airport Bolzano (100 km)
Treviso (170 km)

Arrival From Treviso: take the
A27 to the Belluno exit,
then the SS51 to Cortina
d'Ampezzo. Continue to
San Cassiano via
Falzorego Pass. The hotel
is in town centre beside
the church.

Rosa Alpina

This chic Alpine spa hotel in the tiny village of San Cassiano springs a few surprises. Forget the rich, traditional colours and deep wood panelling you'd expect to find in a chalet-style mountain lodge: here, it's all light and bright as a spring morning, with pale beeswaxed furniture, crisp lines and an impeccably understated style. Creamy-light walls and textured fabrics lend a serenely contemporary air, while antique chests, old paintings and collector's items evoke shades of the region's history. Guests come to ski and snowboard in winter, walk and hike in summer and pursue a multitude of other outdoor pursuits year-round. Indoor pursuits, too, are a must: you can be pummelled and preened into shape in the hotel's spa, where you can plump yourself on a feather-filled sofa in a candlelit room and submit to a cocooning body wrap, facial, herbal steam or aromatherapy massage. This enticing address surrounded by the snow-crusted Dolomites also has another big card up its sleeve: superb Michelin star cuisine under the direction of chef Norbert Niederkopfler, whose talents have made it one of Italy's top restaurants.

Love time   Bedrooms have antique wood floors, ivory bedlinens, copious comforts.
Love bites   Savour healthy, Mediterranean dishes in elegant St Hubertus restaurant.
Love it up   Outdoors? Everything from golf to skiing and mountain biking. Indoors? Shameless pampering includes a milk and honey bath for two.

Bellissimo!   Hit the high notes: peak service in peak surrounds.

Schwarz Adler Turm Hotel
Kirchgasse 2
39040 Cortaccia (Kurtatsch)
T +39 0471 880 600
F +39 0471 880 601
E info@turmhotel.it
W turmhotel.it
Sonia Pomella
24 rooms
Rates €120-170
Dinner from €50

Closed 15 November –15 March

Extras Courtesy of
Room for Romance:
A complimentary bottle
of wine from a local
wine cellar.

Airport Brescia (120 km)

Arrival From Brescia Airport: take
A4 towards Verona, then
A22/E45 till past Trento.
Exit at Montagna for
Cortaccia (Kurtatsch).
Head for town centre;
hotel is just past church.

Schwarz Adler Turm

What a looker. Tucked into a wide valley below the craggy Dolomites in the heart of the South Tyrolean wine route, the Schwarz Adler Turm is a place for all seasons. Visitors are drawn by the changing surrounds, and small wonder. Spring sees nearby apple orchards rioting with pink blossom; summer's heat ensures long days can be spent around the pool with its fabulous valley views; autumn brings russet colours, wine harvests and chestnut picking, with frost lacing trees and hedgerows. The hotel may have been recently built but it faithfully echoes the style of other centuries, fitting snugly with the old village houses in Cortaccia. Easy-on-the-eye, comfortable furnishings and blond wood interiors are redolent of chalet life. As you'd expect here the air is bottle-fresh, but if that's not enough there's also a well-equipped wellness centre with a whirlpool, plunge pool plus treatment rooms (handy after all those rigorous mountain sports). Cooking – enjoyed outside or in, depending on the weather – is given good treatment too. Guests lap up a terrific slice of northern Italian life with a nice helping of Austrian on the side.

Love time   Snuggle-down satisfactions: all rooms embrace a balcony, terrace or loggia.
Love bites   Menus feature trad Tyrolean faves, toothsome puds and quality vinos.
Love it up   Must you have a lie-in? The dramatic Dolomites await with biking, hiking and paragliding, three high-altitude golf courses and skiing.

Bellissimo!   Tyrolean tumbles in Italian setting.

LIGURIA

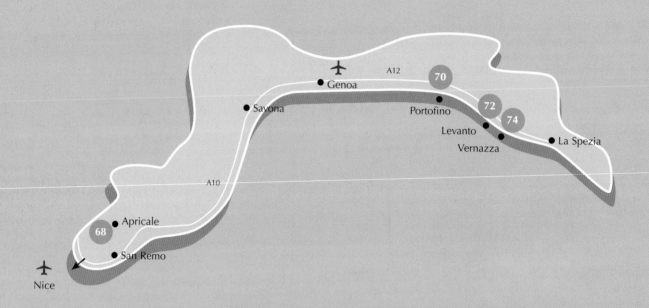

LOVE IT Stretching from the French borders down to Tuscany, Liguria's scenic coastline – all craggy cliffs and plunging wooded slopes – is a winner, while swanky Portofino is the summertime home of Europe's beau monde. **When to go** High summer for the al fresco life and tanning; Easter or mid September for walking on breezy coastal paths. **Don't miss** Walking on the Cinque Terre coastal footpaths, with their fabulous views and overhanging rocks. Musts include the 20-minute stroll along Via dell'Amore between Riomaggiore and Manarola, and the stretch between Corniglia and Vernazza wending among orange and olive groves. Slip into something slinky later for a cocktail or some window-shopping on Portofino's chic waterfront. **Dine on** Fresh Mediterranean seafood is the big thing, while the light and fluffy foccacia is great with local salami. Round off with a slice of Genoan pandolce, stuffed with *frutta candita*. **Drink up** Clinging to steep slopes within spray-shot of the crashing waves, Liguria's vineyards produce some distinctive white wines. Try Sciacchetrà, or a fruity red Ronesse di Dolceacqua.

ITALY'S RIVIERA PLAYGROUND

Pages 68-75

Locanda dei Carugi
Via Roma
18035 Apricale
T +39 0184 209 010
F +39 0184 209 942
E carugi@masterweb.it
W locandadeicarugi.it
Nardo Zaruska
6 rooms
Rates €98-124

Airport   Nice (40 km)

Arrival   From Nice: take the A10 to Ventimiglia. Follow signs for Dolceacqua, Isolabona and Apricale. Park in car park below village; call to arrange luggage assistance (steep hill).

Open all year round

Locanda dei Carugi

Apricale is the kind of too-good-to-be-true medieval hilltop village that surely can't be for real: devastatingly pretty, utterly Italian and virtually undiscovered. Well, pinch yourself hard – we've found it. Well away from the hotspots of the Ligurian Riviera, yet just a short drive inland, it sits atop a hillside in the foothills of the Maritime Alps like a honey-coloured meringue, its terracotta-roofed houses tumbling down the hillside. A narrow lane wiggling between high-sided stone houses leads to a beautiful village square with views across the valley. Locanda dei Carugi is the prettiest B&B perfect for taking all this in, and is crammed with all the character you would expect. There's a delightful breakfast room, where fresh *cornetti* and coffee await in the morning. All six rooms are different, though we loved our top floor quarters, up a spiral staircase with a balcony overlooking a wide valley. Wrought-iron beds with antique wooden headboards and drifts of muslin, hand-painted wooden furniture and pretty lace curtains all add to the idyll. Owner Nardo Zaruska is warmly hospitable and Snoopy the dog will adore you.

Love time   Sleep to the rhythm of an 800-year-old village; wake to the church bells.
Love bites   Some excellent eateries in the village serve unpretentious Ligurian fare.
Love it up   Wander the village streets; stock up for picnics in San Remo's markets; swim in crystal-clear rockpools and waterfalls in nearby Rocchetta Nervina.

Bellissimo! ❧ Pint-size hilltop hideaway in deepest Liguria.

Hotel Splendido
Viale Baratta 16
16034 Portofino
T +39 0185 267 801
F +39 0185 267 806
E reservations@splendido.net
W hotelsplendido.com
Maurizio Saccani
31 rooms, 34 suites
Rates €783-1,332, suites €1,379-4,999
Dinner from €200

Closed mid November – late March

Extras

Courtesy of
Room for Romance:
A complimentary chilled
bottle of sparkling wine in
your room.

Airport

Genoa (37 km)

Arrival

From A12 motorway: exit
at Rapallo and follow
signs to Santa Margherita
and Portofino. Helicopter
landings at Rapallo. Free
shuttle to and from sister
hotel Splendido Mare.

The Splendido

Splendid by name and splendid by nature – that's the Splendido, set in exotic gardens above the millionaire's playground of Portofino. This cachet-laden watering hole of the rich and famous is a grand hotel in every sense, with an illustrious guest list stretching from Humphrey Bogart to the Beckhams. Signed pictures of the vintage Hollywood greats who have stayed line the walls of the lounge. Naturally it's indulgence all the way – assuming your plastic can take the hammering. Rooms are as polished as you'd expect: swish, spacious and oozing a sense of cosseted luxury, right down to the baby-soft bathrobes and the TV and DVD player that pops up at the flick of a switch. Float in the fabulous seawater pool amid rosemary-scented gardens, indulge in spa treatments or gaze down at glamorous Portofino over an al fresco lunch at La Terrazza, clocking the luxury yachts bobbing on the indigo-blue waters of the bay. There's no better place to toast your star-studded address with one of the hotel's trademark bellinis.

Love time   Sea views and a balcony are a must, so there's no point stinting. We loved the deluxe junior suites with their riot of pink flowers.
Love bites   It's breakfast on your terrace, al fresco lunch and candlelit dining at night.
Love it up   Don your shades and hire the hotel's private speedboat, or take the shuttle down to sister property Splendido Mare to browse designer stores.

Bellissimo!   Oscar-winning address in poshest Portofino.

Hotel Stella Maris
Via Marconi 4
19015 Levanto
T +39 0187 808 258
F +39 0187 807 351
E info@hotelstellamaris.it
W hotelstellamaris.it
Renza Pagnini
8 rooms
Rates €200-300
Set menu dinner included in room price

Closed November

Extras   Courtesy of
Room for Romance:
A complimentary glass of
sparkling wine in your
room.

Airport   Pisa (80 km)
Genoa (80 km)

Arrival   From Genoa: take the
A12 to the Carrodano-
Levanto exit. Via Marconi
is in town centre near the
Piazza Cavour. Take trains
from Pisa or Genoa.

Stella Maris

Right at the gates of the fabulous Cinque Terre region – 18 km of near-vertical cliffs, vineyards and terraces – the Stella Maris sits just 100m from the seafront of Levanto, whose beach buzzes with tan-toppers. You'll find it on the first floor of a pinky coloured building dating back to 1850, with additional (more modern) rooms in a nearby house sharing all the Stella's amenities. Owned and managed by Renza Pagnini, the eight-roomed premises exude a homely warmth which belies the magnificent technicolour frescoes racing madly across every ceiling. In fact there's every excuse for lying in bed here: angels, cherubs, knights on white steeds and nymphs are depicted amid clouds and shamelessly OTT spirals of gold on the ceilings above. Throw in antiques, ornately carved wooden furniture, crystal chandeliers and gilded mirrors, and (go on, shut your eyes) you could be in the Sistine chapel's little sister. Renza has won something of a reputation for her food, duly noted by Italian guides; this is served with friendly celebration in a pretty primrose-walled dining room. A landscaped, flower-filled garden provides added scope for outdoor merry-making.

Love time   Look to the heavens: rooms in the main hotel glory under frescoed ceilings.
Love bites   Tuck into Renza's special hand-made pasta, *frittata* and fresh seafood.
Love it up   There are watersports galore and the cliffs of Cinque Terre on the doorstop.

Bellissimo!   Stellar delight on the Ligurian coast.

Trattoria Gianni Franzi
Piazza Marconi 5
19018 Vernazza, Cinque Terre
T +39 0187 821 003
F +39 0187 812 228
E info@giannifranzi.it
W giannifranzi.it
Marisa Gasparini
12 rooms
Rates €65-80
Dinner from €50

Airport   Genoa (90 km)

Arrival   From Genoa: take the
A12/E80 towards La
Spezia. Take exit for
Levanto, then follow signs
for Vernazza.

Closed 10 January – 10 March

Trattoria Gianni Franzi

When top London chefs like Rose Gray and Ruth Rogers – owners of the renowned River Café – start talking about a restaurant, you know it has to be good. Well, here's the place Rogers evidently found inspiration for much of her regional Italian cooking. She and other culinary luminaries have been singing the praises of this seaside trattoria (Sunday Times columnist Michael Winner is another fan), and for good reason. Foodies should make a beeline for this popular family owned restaurant in the Ligurian resort of Vernazza – and the good news is that you can stay here too. Two stone-built houses beneath the castle walls have been turned into a beguiling little hotel perfect for enjoying this part of the glorious Cinque Terre coastline. Make yourselves at home in simply furnished, comfortable rooms with chequered tiled floors, carved wooden beds and artfully chosen paintings. Don't expect posh – it's not – but everything is done up with great taste and style. A grassy terrace perched right above the crashing waves is the perfect spot for afternoon siestas to sleep off a wickedly indulgent lunch.

Love time   Gaze down at the cliffs and foaming waves from Rooms 21 and 22.
Love bites   Look forward to lip-smacking fresh seafood: grilled catch of the day, stuffed mussels, scampi, swordfish and sea urchin.
Love it up   The dramatic Cinque Terre coast awaits with watersports, beaches and trails.

Bellissimo! ▶   Gastronomic good life on a cracking coastline.

MILAN &
THE ITALIAN LAKES

Lake Como
80   84
● Bellagio
S43
82
Lake Garda
Lake Iseo
A1   Como   S342
92   96
86   Bergamo   90
● Monza   94
88   98
78   Milan   ● Brescia
● Pavia   Mantua

LOVE IT Come to Milan – Italy's swish design capital – for shopping, clubbing and retail therapy. Head to the lakes for watersports, fresh air and fabulous surrounds. **When to go** Any time for citybreaks in Milan; June or September for the lakes. **Don't miss** The Giorgio Armani superstore on Milan's Via Manzoni or the original Prada shop in Galleria Vittorio Emanuele. For a cultural fix, admire the white marble Duomo, see Leonardo da Vinci's Last Supper fresco, or buy opera tickets for La Scala. The lakes of Garda, Como and Iseo are the perfect antidote to Milanese city life. Glamorous Como has the jewels of Bellagio and Varenna, Garda has its own mini Riviera around Gardone and Sirmione, while Lake Iseo has its own island – Monte Isola. Chug your way around the lakes on a steamer, calling in at tiny ports. **Dine on** Try costoletta alla milanese – veal chops breaded and fried in butter, or osso buco (braised veal shank). Round off with Milan's most famous dessert – panettone studded with raisins and candied orange peel. **Drink up** Try a local Franciacorta wine and (if you love firewater) a grappa chaser.

CHIC CITY,
COOL WATERS

Pages 78-99

The Straf
Via San Raffaele 3
20121 Milan
T +39 02 805 081
F +39 02 890 95294
E reservations@straf.it
W straf.it
Marco Soli
64 rooms
Rates €246-514

Closed last three weeks of August

Extras

Courtesy of
Room for Romance:
Upgrade with champagne
and strawberries in your
room at a time to suit
you during your stay.

Airport

Milan Linate (10 km)
Milan Malpensa (48 km)
Bergamo (45 km)

Arrival

In Milan: Via San Raffaele
is just off the Piazza del
Duomo; couldn't be
easier to find.

The Straf

Raw, elemental, tactile – this hotel will appeal to those who like their comforts in an expensively stripped-down sort of way. Step from the street through an elaborate 19th century facade into a Japanese-calm space of low sofas and low lighting. Not a frill, flounce or frou-frou in sight; instead, swathes of dark slate, burnished brass, bare cement, textured glass, bold artworks and sober but handsome colours. Black, white and red bedrooms have been pared down to their most seductive basics: a large but simple bed, unobtrusive furniture, mirrored walls, cleverly hidden lights. Decoration is limited to a piece of abstract art, an artfully displayed bamboo twig, a single red apple, and a carelessly tossed throw. It's the perfect, peaceful cocoon. Bathrooms are sumptuous with glittering bronze or gunmetal walls, sculptural white or black basins and huge mirrors. After a hard day's shopping, slink – it's that sort of place – into Straf Bar, a studiedly cool space of industrial art and retro '70s furnishings. One of Milan's classiest hang-outs.

Love time   We adored our 'wellbeing' room, complete with Japanese massage chair, and mood lighting. Won't say what we did with the fab aromatherapy oils.

Love bites   Sleepy lovers can dip their croissants in cappuccino in the breakfast room – a sepulchrally calm space in white and black.

Love it up   Milan's twin temples of designer stores and culture are right at your door.

Bellissimo!   Minimum fuss, maximum pleasure.

Hotel Villa Simplicitas
22028 San Fedele D'Intelvi
Como
T +39 031 831 132
F +39 031 830 455
E info@villasimplicitas.it
W villasimplicitas.it
Ulla Wagner
10 rooms
Rates €80-120
Dinner from €60

Closed November – March

Extras Courtesy of
Room for Romance:
A welcome aperitif on
arrival.

Airport Milan Malpensa (50 km)
Bergamo (60 km)
Milan Linate (70 km)

Arrival From Milan: take the A9
north, exit at Como Nord,
follow signs to Menaggio
then San Fedele Intelvi.
Cross main square and
follow hotel signs.

Villa Simplicitas

This primrose-yellow house with green shutters is set on a leafy hillside among meadows and chestnut trees. The 19th century villa lies midway between Lakes Como and Lugano, with sweeping views of rugged Alpine foothills. This is a country house full of antiques and rugs, sometimes faded but full of character and charm. The sitting room has a huge open fireplace and is crammed with objets d'art, turn-of-the-century lamps and period paintings. There's even a billiard room – something of a rarity in Italy – with the original baize table. Upstairs, bedrooms have wrought-iron or brass bedsteads, free-standing wardrobes and chunky chests of drawers. It's all a million miles away from today's stripped-down functionality, and betrays more than a hint of nostalgia for times past. A far more recent addition is the glass-covered terrace at the rear (be sure to grab a window seat) where you can drink in panoramic views of Lake Lugano along with a bottle or two of fine Chianti. Outside, the heady scent of hydrangeas, meadow grass and linden trees is mountain-fresh. The two resident shaggy dogs will happily join you on a stroll through the woods – and for a change of scene, you're just a two-mile hop from Switzerland.

Love time	Choose one of the two bedrooms with a terrace for fabulous views.
Love bites	Candlelit dinners on the terrace with hearty Lombardy cuisine are a treat.
Love it up	Nearby there's riding, tennis and golf, plus lakes Como and Lugano.

Pleasing villa in tranquil lakeland setting.

La Pergola
Piazza del Porto 4, Pescallo
22021 Bellagio
T +39 031 950 263
F +39 031 950 253
E info@lapergolabellagio.it
W lapergolabellagio.it
Livio Gatti
11 rooms
Rates €105-300
Dinner from €40

Extras — Courtesy of Room for Romance: A complimentary chilled bottle of sparkling wine in your room.

Airport — Bergamo (42 km)

Arrival — Head to Bellagio. From the North, Pescallo is signposted on the right just before Bellagio itself, or from the South skirt around top of Bellagio then take left turn to Pescallo.

Closed November – March

La Pergola

In the shape of an inverted 'Y,' Lake Como is the deepest and most dramatic of all the Italian northern lakes. For many it is also the most romantic. Cradled between the two arms of the 'Y' is Bellagio – Como's jewel. A ten minute walk away through a tangle of cobbled streets is the tiny fishing village of Pescallo, where you'll find La Pergola. Pretty in pink with a vine-clad terrace overlooking the lake, this 16th century building was once a nunnery. Today the family-run little treasure has a devoted following of those addicted to more sybaritic pursuits. We loved Pescallo: it has a timeless quality that makes you feel as if you're in your own private little Italian village.The hotel and its rooms are basic, with tiled floors, low-vaulted ceilings and fans. Bedrooms vary in size, their old furniture married with modern beds and bathrooms. But what makes La Pergola so special is the peerless location and excellent food. We took a ringside seat by the lake and (along with numerous regulars) greedily devoured some of the local fishermen's catch. When the sun sets and lights twinkle over the lake, it's romance in spades. Get thee to a nunnery, anyone?

Love time	Ask for the balconied rooms on the upper floors for the best views.
Love bites	The vine-canopied terrace is just the spot to enjoy home-cooked Italian specialities: local mushrooms, cheese, *verdure al forno* or polenta.
Love it up	Buy something slinky and silky from Como – Italy's silk capital.

Bellissimo!	Little gem with a lot to shout about.

Albergo Milano
Via XX Settembre 29
23829 Varenna
T +39 0341 830 298
F +39 0341 830 061
E hotelmilano@varenna.net
W varenna.net
Bettina & Egidio Mallone
8 rooms
Rates €130-145
Dinner from €50

Open March – November

Extras Courtesy of
Room for Romance:
A welcome glass of
prosecco on
arrival.

Airport Bergamo (50 km)
Milan Linate (72 km)

Arrival Once in Varenna itself
the hotel is signposted.
Via XX Settembre is just
off the main street in
the heart of the old
town.

Albergo Milano

Set against a backdrop of Alpine grandeur, Lake Como drips romance. Varenna's pastel-painted houses cluster around a church on the rocky shoreline and narrow cobbled streets lead to the waterfront and the cappuccino-coloured Albergo. Disarmingly small with just eight bedrooms, this gorgeous little place is simply yet stylishly furnished, and the warmth of the welcome matches its mellow rusticity. But as well as the owners Bettina and Egidio, the stars here are the spectacular views. Each bedroom has a balcony or terrace overlooking the rippling waters of the lake, with a different colour scheme and individually designed tiled floors, carefully matched to the 150-year-old originals. The airy lobby has an invitingly cosy chimney corner and the wide windows of the aptly named La Vista restaurant and terrace offer breathtaking views over the lake. When Egidio isn't creating gastronomic delights in the kitchen, he and his wife create the perfect spot for incurable romantics to indulge in their hotel motto – *dolce far niente*. The sweet delight of doing nothing.

Love time	Rooms 1 and 2 have huge terraces – perfect for sipping a glass of bubbly.
Love bites	Enjoy a specially prepared picnic hamper for two, or savour Egidio's culinary delights from the scenic restaurant terrace.
Love it up	A boat trip across the lake will take you to Bellagio, Como's jewel.

Lakeland gem with dreamy views.

Casa Clelia
Via Corna 1/3
24039 Sotto il Monte
T +39 035 799 133
F +39 035 791 788
E info@casaclelia.com
W casaclelia.com
Rosanna Minonzio
10 rooms
Rates €85-120
Dinner from €58

Airport   Bergamo (18 km)
Milan Linate (35 km)

Arrival   From Bergamo: take A4
and exit at Capriate.
Follow signs for Suisio,
Calusco, then Sotto il
Monte. Watch for little
'piggy' signposts to hotel.

Open all year round

Casa Clelia

Narrow roads wind up to this rustic 17th century manor house – a former medieval convent – tucked up in the hills. There's a farm alongside with a kitchen garden, stables and flocks of clucking chickens, and the warmest welcome from owner Rosanna. We loved the old wooden dressers laden with home-made jams, gleaming vegetables in oil, hams and salami in the entrance hall. A huge stone fireplace is the centrepiece of the rustic Il Camino restaurant, whose exposed stonework, barrel vaults and wood floors make it tailor-made for candlelit dinners. Each ample bedroom has a painted flower fairy on the door (no anonymous room numbers here), with polished wood floors, open beams, stonework and bright splashes of colour. Eco-friendliness is a top priority here, and heating comes from wood-burning stoves and solar panels, while jute and cork panelling ensure – should your ardour get the better of you – effective sound-proofing. Roomy bathrooms, some with roll-top baths and huge basins, are stylish and softly lit.

Love time	The Gerbera suite comes in hot colours with an open fireplace.
Love bites	Look forward to wonderful home-cooked organic food. We tucked into asparagus risotto, roasted vegetables and delicious home-made bread.
Love it up	Stroll beneath wisteria and jasmine amid the rustlings of nature. There's riding and cycling nearby, plus Le Cornelle Animal Park.

Hens, horses, haylofts… just right for country guys and gals.

L'Albereta
Via Vittorio Emanuele II 23
25030 Erbusco
T +39 030 776 0550
F +39 030 776 0573
E info@albereta.it
W albereta.it
48 rooms, 9 suites
Rates €230-490, suites €430-900
Dinner from €90

Restaurant closed January 2 – February 8

Extras

Courtesy of
Room for Romance:
A complimentary bottle
of Franciacorta wine
in your room.

Airport

Bergamo (69 km)

Arrival

From Milan: take the
A4 motorway towards
Venice. Take the Rovato
exit then follow signs to
Sarnico-Erbusco. This
road leads directly into
the village.

L'Albereta

Set among vineyards deep in the Lombardy countryside, this former hunting lodge (where you can expect to bump into a few Milanese fashionistas) is now dedicated to hunters of the five c's: *cortesia, carattere, calma, charme* and *cucina*. L'Albereta scores on every count. This ivy-clad retreat is the ancestral villa of the Moretti family and packed with antiques and museum-quality art. Huge sculptures adorn the manicured grounds and you can almost pluck the fruit of the vines from your room. Decor is rustically traditional and period frescoes alternate with airy provençal touches. Rooms – some with canopied beds, fireplaces and rich tapestries – are lavishly detailed. Some of the marble bathrooms have jacuzzis and intimate saunas à deux. The airy restaurant is a temple to gourmet cuisine with two Michelin stars awarded to famous Italian chef Gualtiero Marchesi. His superb dishes are reason enough to make the pilgrimage here along with many glitterati – not forgetting the luxury Espace Vitalité wellness centre overseen by French spa guru Henri Chenot, whose mantra is the rediscovery of harmony and energy. Great recipe for love.

Love time   The Lake Tower suite has a retractable roof for star-gazing – sleeping optional.

Love bites   Chef Gualtiero Marchesi's gastronomy marries superb seasonal produce with creative flair. This is definitely an adult's culinary pleasure ground.

Love it up   Drink in the vineyard views with Lake Iseo glinting in the distance.

Bellissimo!   This feast for the senses should come with an addictive warning.

Relais I Due Roccoli
Colline di Iseo, Via Silvio Bonomelli
25049 Iseo
T +39 030 982 2977
F +39 030 982 2980
E relais@idueroccoli.com
W idueroccoli.com
Vincento Agoni
13 Rooms
Rates €149-190
Dinner from €100

Closed 1 November – 15 March

Extras Courtesy of
Room for Romance:
A complimentary chilled
bottle of champagne in
your room.

Airport Bergamo (20 km)

Arrival From A4 Milan-Venice
highway: take exit for
Rovato, then Iseo.
Near Iseo turn right
immediately after two
tunnels towards Polavero;
hotel is 4.5 km further.

I Due Roccoli

Overshadowed by its bigger, brasher neighbours of Como and Garda, Lake Iseo is little-known outside Italy. Perched high above its south-eastern shores, with vine-clad hills to the south and mountains rising from the western slopes, I Due Roccoli takes full advantage of the lake's lesser-known charms. A handsome country villa set in acres of gardens and wooded parkland, it has uninterrupted views of the lake while the only sound here is birdsong. The style is classic Italian country house; soft colours, antique furniture, oil paintings and grand fireplaces, with the emphasis on comfort rather than ostentation. Spacious bedrooms, some with raftered ceilings, come with a terrace or balcony and floor-to-ceiling windows to make the best of those stunning views. The cooking here is first rate, so be sure to nab a table in the elegant dining room or candlelit terrace to enjoy fine Franciacorta wines, fresh lake-caught fish and some of the best of Lombard cuisine. Cool off in the pool, practice your ground strokes on the tennis court, kip beneath a shady tree or simply clock those terrific views.

Love time	Lake views, breakfast on your terrace: definitely worth getting out of bed for.
Love bites	Prepare to go the full Monty: from antipastis and primis through to wicked puds, these are dinners you'll want to do justice to.
Love it up	Walk round the lake, visit Iseo's Friday market, watch the sun go down.

Bellissimo! Unspoilt views, utterly spoiling surroundings.

Hotel du Lac
Via Colletta 21
25084 Villa di Gargnano, Lake Garda
T +39 0365 71107 (winter only: 71269)
F +39 0365 71055
E info@hotel-dulac.it
W hotel-dulac.it
The Arosio family
12 rooms
Rates €84-120
Dinner from €60

Airport
Brescia (45 km)
Verona (75 km)
Bergamo (90 km)

Arrival
From A4 Milan-Venice
motorway: exit at Brescia
Est/Lago di Garda
Occidentale. Follow
signs for Salò, Toscolano,
Maderno and Gargnano.
Turn right into Via Colletta
400m after Bogliaco.
Free public parking
100m from hotel.

Closed November – Early April

Hotel du Lac

"The lake lies dim and milky, the mountains dark blue at the back, while over them the sky gushes and glistens with light." It was in Gargnano, on the shores of Lake Garda, that DH Lawrence penned these words while writing Twilight in Italy. Literary stuff indeed. This 1920s townhouse with a striking terracotta facade, just along the road from the Villa Igea where Lawrence stayed, still oozes period charm. The Arosio family home until 1959, little has changed since it was turned into a hotel – still family-run, with mellow old-fashioned furniture, 1930s lights, Persian rugs, antiques and polished terrazzo floors. The lake is so close that you can swim straight off the overhanging patio, and the family go out of their way to make you feel at home. Six of the rooms look out onto the lake and have small balconies. Dine in La Bissa restaurant, set around a central courtyard with a great palm soaring up into the clear skies and panoramic windows overlooking the water, or dine upstairs on a divine open terrace shaded by an arbour of kiwi. Then serenade each other on the music room's piano before beddy-byes.

Love time   Gaze at lakeside lights twinkling from your balcony under balmy night skies.
Love bites   Candlelight, lake views and crisp white linen are the backdrop to a menu featuring home-made pasta and lake-fresh fish.
Love it up   Nearby are watersports galore, Villa Romana and day trips to Venice.

Old-world charmer in a picture-worthy setting.

Hotel Gardenia al Lago
Via Colletta 53
25084 Villa di Gargnano, Lake Garda
T +39 0365 71195 (winter only: 71269)
F +39 0365 72594
E info@hotel-gardenia.it
W hotel-gardenia.it
The Arosio family
25 rooms
Rates €70-206
Dinner from €60

Closed November – early April

Airport Brescia (45 km)
Verona (75 km)
Bergamo (90 km)

Arrival From Milan-Venice A4 highway: exit at Brescia Est/Lago di Garda Occidentale. Follow signs for Salò, Toscolano, Maderno and Gargnano. Go right 400m after village of Bogliaco into Via Colletta. Private parking.

Gardenia al Lago

You can imagine Victorian travellers standing in awe on the shores of Lake Garda, taking in all that glittering blue water, green wooded shores and little houses painted in rainbow pastels. Little has changed: stand on the terrace of Gardenia al Lago – the summer home of the Arosio family since 1925 – and you'll be smitten by those same charms. This handsome villa, its gardens brushing the water's edge, has scarcely changed either. Turned into a hotel in the 1950s, it still retains shades of the period while refurbishment ensures today's guests lap up every comfort. Airy, welcoming rooms have burnished mahogany bedsteads, polished terrazzo floors and – in some – French doors opening onto a private balcony or terrace. Dining here is a treat – especially when fine weather sees tables spread through the lush gardens, where palm trees flutter, to make the most of the captivating views. There's no better place to idle away a deliciously lazy afternoon than the scenic terrace set with sunloungers, where you can soak up the rays or gaze at snow-capped Monte Baldo.

Love time	Invite lakeshore breezes in: choose a room with a view and your own terrace.
Love bites	Start the day with breakfast shaded by olive and bay trees in the gardens. Finish with dinner by candleglow, watching lights twinkle across the water.
Love it up	Go straight for the Blue: try kayaking, kite surfing, sailing or diving.

Bellissimo! Garda charmer that's a pure tonic.

Locanda San Verolo
37010 Costermano
Lake Garda
T +39 045 720 0930
F +39 045 620 1166
E info@sanverolo.it
W sanverolo.it
Dagmar Gufler
8 rooms
Rates €280-330
Dinner from €35

Closed November – March

Extras

Courtesy of
Room for Romance:
A basket of seasonal
fresh fruit in your
room.

Airport

Verona (35 km)
Brescia (40 km)

Arrival

From Verona: take A22 in
direction of Brennero. Exit
at Affi-Lago di Garda Sud.
Follow signs to Costermano
then to San Verolo, where
the hotel is signed.

Locanda San Verolo

Hidden behind a high stone wall, you could slip by this farmhouse and scarcely notice it. But step through the gateway and you're in for a treat. High above the eastern shore of Lake Garda in the village of Costermano, this handsome, blue-shuttered building has been converted into a luxury inn with rooms. Great care has been taken to preserve original 16th and 17th century features – polished floor tiles, dark beams, rough plaster walls – and seamlessly blend them with a classically, understated style. Creamy walls, flowing curtains and soft rugs mix with boldly striped sofas and hand-painted furniture to create a rich but relaxing atmosphere. There are thoughtful touches – fat white candles, elegant writing desks – while the bathrooms are no-holds barred, decadent, blood-red and white marble fantasies. Just the place for a lingering soak with a glass of prosecco. Should you tear yourselves away, there is not one but two pools. Lie back on a white-cushioned sunlounger, gaze down at your lakeside surrounds or up to the distinctive tip of Monte Baldo in the distance and congratulate yourself on your clever find.

Love time   The bedroom under the eaves with the roll-top bathtub was our favourite.
Love bites Dine under the awnings on homely but stylish cooking with Bardolino wines.
Love it up Lounge on the private beach at Punta San Vigilio, a tree-cloaked promontory on Lake Garda, or take the cable car up Monte Baldo.

A rare little find you'll want to keep to yourself.

Locanda San Vigilio
37016 Garda
Lake Garda
T +39 045 725 6688
F +39 045 725 6551
E info@punta-sanvigilio.it
W punta-sanvigilio.it
Christine Weder
7 rooms, 3 suites
Rates €235-310
Dinner from €90

Closed November – March

Extras Courtesy of
Room for Romance:
A basket of seasonal
fresh fruit in your room.

Airport Verona (30 km)
Brescia (40 km)

Arrival From Verona: take the
A22 towards Brennero.
Exit at Affi-Lago di Garda
Sud and follow signs to
Garda, then to Torri. San
Vigilio is 4 km outside
Garda.

Locanda San Vigilio

Through half-closed eyes, you could be on your own private island. The finger of tree-cloaked land that lies languidly in the cool blue of Lake Garda is virtually surrounded by water. At the end of its cypress-lined avenue, a cobbled street leads to a tiny harbour and a powder-pink, blue-shuttered inn that has been welcoming guests since the 16th century. Apart from a small taverna, a secluded villa and an ancient church, there are no other buildings – or people – to spoil the views. This is all about grand and comfortable Italian country house living; the style Laurence Olivier and Vivien Leigh would (indeed, did) enjoy. Vast rooms have thick carpets on polished wood floors, silk bedcovers, oil paintings, ornate carved bedheads and heavy antiques glowing in the soft lights. Bathrooms are full of old-fashioned luxuries, heavy with marble and masses of towels. And the suites, darling, are even grander. Wander through the garden, breathe in the scent of lemon trees, or just take it lazy beneath an olive tree on the private beach. Come evening, sip an *aperitivo* at the harbourside taverna and watch the sun set over the lake.

Love time	Spoil yourselves in the Grand suite with its 16th century four-poster.
Love bites	Sit down to white napery and soft candles; ask for a window seat and you'll feel you're floating above the water.
Love it up	Explore the lake by motorboat, go windsurfing, or tan on the private beach.
Bellissimo!	A serene spot in a lakeland landscape.

EMILIA-ROMAGNA

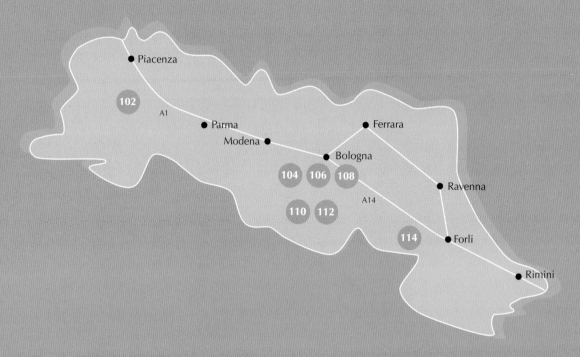

LOVE IT Parma ham, Parmesan cheese, Mortadella sausage, ravioli, tortelloni... they all come from Emilia-Romagna, nicknamed the belly of Italy. Come here to eat, drink and be merry – this region produces some of the world's greatest food and wines. **When to go** Any time for Bologna (though some hotels close in August); summer and autumn (when the truffle season is in full swing) for the country. **Don't miss** This is the place for gastro-tours: visit wine cellars, cheese producers, pasta factories and working farms. There are wine routes to follow and gourmet festivals to join in, not to mention three national parks to explore. People-watch on Bologna's Piazza Maggiore and take a look at Le Due Torri – the old leaning towers, before browsing the city's famous markets, delis and food halls. **Dine on** Truffles, porcini mushrooms and pasta every which way you like it are part of the region's celebrated cuisine – just avoid restaurants serving up spaghetti Bolognese; it's strictly for the tourists. **Drink up** Go *frizzante* here – raise a frothy glass of purply-pink Lambrusco wine, or try some of the region's easy whites and zesty reds.

ART, WINE &
GASTRONOMY

Pages 102-115

Villa Bellaria
Via Dei Gasperini 6
29010 Cortina di Alseno
T +39 0523 947 537
F +39 338 692 5674
E info@villabellariabb.it
W villabellariabb.it
Marina Cazzaniga Calderoni
3 rooms
Rates €60-70

Open all year round

Extras

Courtesy of
Room for Romance:
A welcome drink
on arrival.

Airport

Milan Linate (90 km)
Bergamo (100 km)

Arrival

From Milan: take the A1
towards Bologna, exit at
Fiorenzuola, then take the
SS9 in direction of Parma.
After Alseno, turn right at
traffic lights and follow
signs after 5 km.

Villa Bellaria

With only three rooms in this little villa, you might even find you have it all to yourselves. It's surrounded by well-lawned gardens and brilliant views of the Piacenza hills, and is within easy reach of three of Italy's most famous spa towns. Even if you're not alone you'll still feel deliciously far from the madding crowd and enjoy owner Marina Calderoni's full attention. The place is furnished like a home, meaning it's warm, comfortable and inviting. Modern pictures and prints line the walls of the sitting room, with its cobalt blue sofas, while wrought-iron beds and creamy-pale bedspreads make bedrooms worth retiring to. In winter a log fire adds further cosiness. In summer French doors open onto a long paved patio, shaded and cooled by a colonnaded roof. Tables and chairs are at the ready and a hammock slung between two posts encourages idleness. This little place makes an ideal roost when you don't want to meet the demands of fancier places. Come here to loll around, soak up the surrounds over a bottle or two of local Barbera wine and enjoy the area's rustic cuisine. Great tranquilliser!

Love time   Kick off your shoes and play rock-a-bye baby in the hammock.
Love bites   Tuck into Marina's delicious breakfasts on the shady patio in summer.
Love it up   Check out the medieval villages of Vigoleno and Castell'Arquato; try the spa waters at Salsomaggiore; get golfing at the club next door.

Bellissimo! ❤   Pint-size B&B made for gentle R&R.

Hotel Al Cappello Rosso
Via de'Fusari 9 (Piazza Maggiore)
40123 Bologna
T +39 051 261 891
F +39 051 227 179
E info@alcappellorosso.it
W alcappellorosso.it
Lucien Pilot
33 rooms
Rates €200-410

Closed for two weeks in August

Extras   Courtesy of
Room for Romance:
A bottle of champagne
and breakfast in your
room. Special gift if
staying for Valentine's Day.

Airport   Bologna (5 km)
Forlì (66 km)

Arrival   The hotel is right in the
city centre, a stone's
throw from the Piazza
Maggiore. Main rail
station: 2 km.

Al Cappello Rosso

In a city stuffed with history, it's no surprise to hear that the origins of Al Cappello Rosso stretch back over 600 years. Things couldn't be more different today, however. If you'd sooner keep the city's olde-worlde charms outside the door, you'll be glad that top-to-bottom refurbishment has transformed the Cappello into sleek and modern quarters bursting with contemporary good looks. Inside, expect shades of Conran: signature notes include black raffia chairs, square-sided sofas, gleaming tiled floors and tall plants. Bold reds, wide mirrors, downlighters and well-kitted out bathrooms characterise the bedrooms, while solid walls ensure you won't know what your fellow guests are up to. Wrap yourselves in cool his n' hers kimonos and just take it easy. There's also a striking, glass-ceilinged breakfast room where black and cream are used to stylish effect. The hotel has a decent bar, obliging staff who know how to make you feel welcome and – just yards from Piazza Maggiore – it's close to all the action.

Love time	The mansard suite's garret windows offer a great outlook on the old city.
Love bites	You won't be short of dining spots: with its rich culinary heritage, Bologna isn't known as La Grassa (the fat one) for nothing.
Love it up	Reclaim the past by checking out Le Due Torre (the leaning towers) and a host of churches and basilicas.

Bellissimo! 🗲 Sleek spot hits the spot in ancient spot.

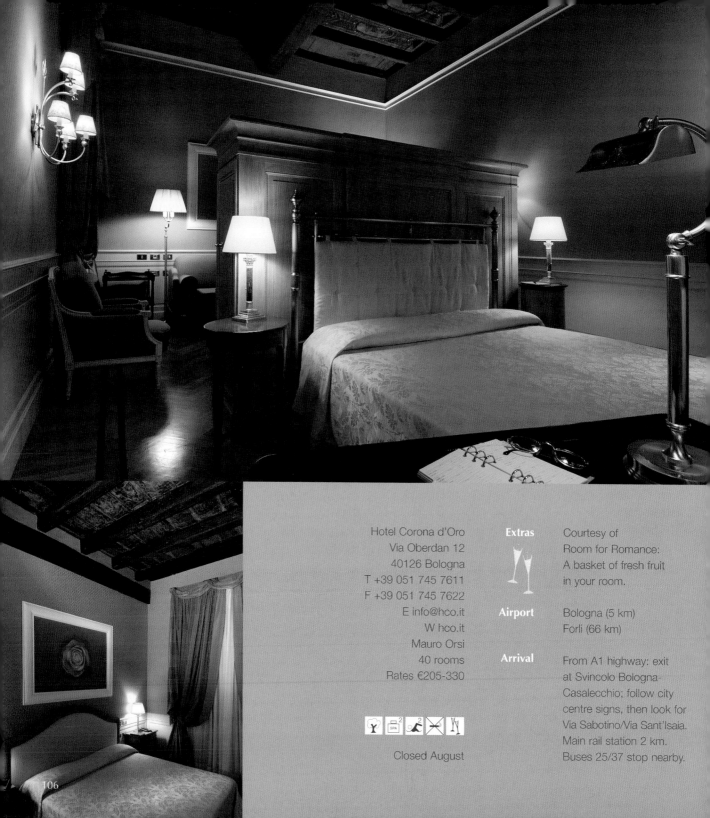

Hotel Corona d'Oro
Via Oberdan 12
40126 Bologna
T +39 051 745 7611
F +39 051 745 7622
E info@hco.it
W hco.it
Mauro Orsi
40 rooms
Rates €205-330

Closed August

Extras

Courtesy of
Room for Romance:
A basket of fresh fruit
in your room.

Airport

Bologna (5 km)
Forli (66 km)

Arrival

From A1 highway: exit
at Svincolo Bologna-
Casalecchio; follow city
centre signs, then look for
Via Sabotino/Via Sant'Isaia.
Main rail station 2 km.
Buses 25/37 stop nearby.

Hotel Corona d'Oro

The outside is intriguing, the interior a revelation. The medieval arcaded entrance, down a quiet street in the heart of the city, leads not into a dimly lit hallway but into a stunningly light and white Art Nouveau salon. Originally a 13th century palazzo, the building has undergone many changes. Here you might find a coffered ceiling, over there a medieval fresco, while elsewhere are beautiful flourishes of Art Nouveau stucco work. Sounds odd but works a dream. The original inner courtyard has been boldly glassed over to create the light-filled lounge where you can sink into white sofas and enjoy an espresso – or prosecco, if it's that time of day – with some deliciously dainty cakes. A red-carpeted, white marble staircase sweeps up to the bedrooms. No two are the same. Some might have frescoes, others a painted ceiling, some have dado panelling, others rooftop views of Bologna. All have been subtly modernised with classically understated furnishings – pale parquet floors, rich fabrics, silk bedspreads – with bold modern art and marble bathrooms. All this, and you're right in the heart of one of Italy's most fabulous cities.

Love time	Choose one of the suites – all taffeta drapes and painted raftered ceilings.
Love bites	Breakfast in exotic surrounds: crimson walls hung with Art Nouveau lamps.
Love it up	Elegant shops in Via Oberdan are a mere stiletto hop away; when you're spent out, strut your stuff in nearby Piazza del Nettuno.
Bellissimo!	Medieval palazzo with an artful twist.

Art Hotel Novecento
Piazza Galilei 4/3
40126 Bologna
T +39 051 745 7311
F +39 051 745 7322
E novecento@inbo.it
W bolognarthotels.it
Mauro and Cristina Orsi
25 rooms
Rates €195-330

Closed August

Extras Courtesy of
Room for Romance:
A basket of fresh fruit in
your room.

Airport Bologna (5 km)
Forli (66 km)

Arrival From A1 highway: exit at
Svincolo Bologna-
Casalecchio; follow city
centre signs, then look for
Via Sabotino/Via Sant'Isaia.
Main rail station 2 km.
Buses 25/37 stop nearby.

Art Hotel Novecento

This boldly contemporary address in the heart of medieval Bologna – the city's newest boutique hotel – has won rave reviews since opening in 2003. Owners Mauro and Cristina Orsi have given their latest Bolognese protégé a decidedly cutting-edge feel, gutting an early 20th century city townhouse to create chic and pared-down quarters with shades of 1930s Vienna. It's all beautifully understated and done with faultless taste. Spacious, spotless rooms – some with windows framing the spires and towers of the old city – sport bold artworks, mahogany headboards, slick lighting, expensive linens and Asian-inspired screens and mirrors. Bathrooms with his 'n hers bathrobes are tiled in desert-storm hued Jerusalem marble. Mansard windows in the beautiful top floor rooms – done out in a duet of whites – capture snapshots of the churches, belfries and palazzi outside. The lounge bar is just the place for drinks at the end of the day. Sat in a tranquil sidestreet just west of Piazza Maggiore – Bologna's social heart – Art Hotel Novecento is perfectly positioned for taking in the sights of this fascinating city.

Love time   Strictly modern bedrooms come with firm beds and fab bathrooms with plenty of lotions on the side.

Love bites   Some of Bologna's best-known restaurants are within walking distance.

Love it up   People-watch in Piazza Maggiore; spend in unashamedly swanky shops.

Bellissimo! ➤   Bolognese boutique address brimming with style.

La Fenice
Via San Lucia 29, Ca' de Gatti
40040 Rocca di Roffeno
T +39 051 919 272
F +39 051 919 024
E lafenice@lafeniceagritur.it
W lafeniceagritur.it
Remo and Paolo Giarandoni
9 rooms
Rates €80-120
Dinner from €40

Closed 10 January – 10 February

Extras   Courtesy of
Room for Romance:
An upgrade to the best
available room.

Airport   Bologna (40 km)

Arrival   From Bologna: Take the
tangenziale (ring road)
going south towards
Casalecchio, Maranello
and Tolè. Continue for
2 km past Tolè, from
where the hotel is
signposted.

La Fenice

Bedded in woods high in the hills south of Bologna, this 16th century country farmhouse is the place to get back to nature. Leafy-green surrounds and mountain-fresh air induce total relaxation, and – unless you fancy lending a hand with the harvest – relaxing is just what it's all about. This is a place to devour your holiday paperbacks in a deckchair, splash in the pool, walk on forest trails and soak up ever-present hillside views. Bedrooms are simple and country-cosy with raftered ceilings and shuttered windows. After a day in the great outdoors you're sure to have an appetite, and hearty regional cooking awaits. Candles, rustic decor and a crackling fire on cooler evenings add intimacy to the friendly restaurant, where locally bred pork is a favourite. Tuck into the grilled pork fillet with balsamic vinegar – or, in season, black and white truffles, porcini mushrooms and other local specialities. Feeling energetic? Sign up for some riding lessons: there's great pony trekking hereabouts and you'll see places only accessible on foot or on horseback. Brothers Remo and Paolo ensure a warm welcome.

Love time	The roomy Caminetto suite has its own stone fireplace.
Love bites	Delicious starters include tagliatelle with wild herbs and pancetta.
Love it up	Go pony trekking, pedal off on mountain bikes, take aim at archery or get ready for take-off in a hang glider.

Bellissimo! ▶ Country air, country beds, country life.

La Piana dei Castagni
Via Lusignano 11
40040 Rocca di Roffeno
T +39 051 912 985
F +39 051 912 985
E info@pianadeicastagni.it
W pianadeicastagni.it
Valeria Vitali
5 rooms
Rates €75
Dinner from €45

Closed December – February

Extras

Courtesy of
Room for Romance:
A bottle of local sparkling
wine, flowers and candles
in your room.

Airport

Bologna (40 km)

Arrival

From Bologna: take A1
for Florence, then S64 to
Pian di Venolo. Follow
signs for Vedegheto, Tolè,
Santa Lucia, Bocco Ravari.
Follow hotel signs from
Torre Jussi.

La Piana dei Castagni

The point about coming to this comfortably converted 19th century farmhouse high above a valley with views of the Tuscan-Emilia hills is to forget it all. Guests come here to dump the stressful baggage and switch on to the simple life. The mellow stone building reached along a winding track sprinkled with leafy chestnut trees (hence its name) may look a modest starting point, but the serenity herabouts and the warmth of owner Valeria Vitali lend it lashings of down-on-the-farm appeal. This is somewhere to idle, read or paint the vistas around you from the terrace and sunny courtyard, with its climbing roses, or to potter round local markets, go truffle-hunting and set off on breezy country treks. You're within reach of three national parks here, not to mention working farms where parmesan cheeses, balsamic vinegar and fine Appenine wines are produced. There's a lively fire during cooler months in the farmhouse's sunnily painted dining room, while simply decorated bedrooms in restful pastels, with rustic prints and bedcovers, are made for curled-up nights.

Love time	Fling open the windows to valley views and get that back-to-nature feel.
Love bites	Dinners are cooked to order – look forward to traditional Emilian house specialities like tigelle montanare, tortelloni alle ortiche and torta de riso.
Love it up	Take in medieval villages and farms, or Florence and Bologna for a city fix.

Bellissimo! ➤ Hilltop B&B where it's back to the good life.

Relais Torre Pratesi
Via Cavina 11
48013 Brisighella
T +39 0546 84545
F +39 0546 84558
E info@torrepratesi.it
W torrepratesi.it
Letizia and Nerio Raccagni
9 rooms
Rates €150-180
Dinner from €45

Open all year round

Extras

Airport

Arrival

Courtesy of
Room for Romance:
A complimentary bottle of
sparkling wine in your
room.

Forli (35 km)

From Bologna: take S9
towards Forli, then S302
towards Brisighella at
Faenza. At Fognano turn
right into Via della
Lavando then bear left
into Via Cavina for hotel.

Torre Pratesi

Why not flee to the remote and scenic hills of Romagna to bunker down in a tall 16th century fortified watchtower... where you'll be willing prisoners of Nerio and Letizia Raccagni's hospitality. They encourage a sociable house-party atmosphere, and today's fortifying comes strictly from their farm and kitchen garden, fed in turn by the region's vineyards and larder (you can spot boar, elk, roe deer and pheasant in the woods). The four-storey stone tower houses four atmospheric oak-beamed suites, each occupying an entire floor. Next to it is a flower bordered farmhouse with more suites, and some cottages. Traditional stone, beamed ceilings, tiled floors splashed with rugs and wrought-iron bedsteads lend the interiors plenty of rustic charm. There's an inviting lounge with leather armchairs, shelves of books and a huge stone fireplace, together with a bar with complimentary drinks. Outside, the grounds and surrounds invite you to get back to nature. Visit the farm animals, admire views of Monte Maggiore or set off for the day with a bike, a steed or some golf clubs.

Love time   Take the top-floor Del Falco suite, with 360 degree views all to yourselves.
Love bites   Only home-grown and local produce goes into the pot. Candlelit dinners feature Letizia's terrific cooking and farm-made cheeses, jams and patés.
Love it up   Go biking, hiking or riding in glorious rolling terrain.

Bellissimo! ✎   Tuscan-style tower you'll relish being banished to.

FLORENCE
& TUSCANY

Viareggio
172
A11
Lucca
Pisa
142
Florence
144
170
S2
A1
San Gimignano
146
168
Arezzo
Siena
148
166 164
150
E78
Cortona
S1
158
152
Montepulciano
160
154
162
156
Giglio
S1

118 120 122 124 126 128
130 132 134 136 138 140

LOVE IT Tailor-made for a cultural pick-me-up, Tuscany can't be beaten for its wealth of art treasures and history. Bursting with medieval masterpieces, it's also stuffed with vineyards, ancient stone farmhouses and those classic rolling hills. This is Italy with all its bells and whistles. **When to go** Try autumn or winter, when it's crisp and crowd-free. **Don't miss** Make the most of the culture factor. Florence has a banquet of Renaissance treasures: Michelangelo's David, the Ponte Vecchio, the Uffizi (the world's oldest art gallery) and the fabulous Duomo. Other Tuscan gems include medieval Siena, atmospheric San Gimignano, with its stone towers, Montepulciano, Cortona and Pienza. **Dine on** Game – often served with canellini beans, tonno e fagioli – tuna fish and beans – and pollo al brunello, a tasty winter chicken stew. Be sure to crunch into some delicious panforte – Siena's sweet-tooth dessert. **Drink up** You'll want to quaff Chianti, Tuscany's most famous export, as well as its more full-bodied cousins like Brunello di Montalcino. Round off with a nocino, a bitter-sweet walnut liqueur.

HEART OF RENAISSANCE ITALY

Pages 118-173

Palazzo Magnani Feroni
Borgo San Frediano 5
50124 Florence
T +39 055 2399 544
F +39 055 2608 908
E info@palazzomagnaniferoni.com
W florencepalace.it
Alberto Giannotti
12 rooms
Rates €210-750

Open all year round

Extras   Courtesy of
Room for Romance:
A welcome cocktail on
arrival.

Airport   Florence (4 km)
Pisa (80 km)

Arrival   Go south over the Ponte
alla Carraia, walk down
Serragli, and turn right
into Borgo San Frediano.

Palazzo Magnani Feroni

Like a rich plum pudding, Florence bursts with art treasures: the Uffizi and dell'Accademia among them. The 16th century Palazzo Magnani Feroni is less public but equally awesome. Walk back into an age of grand living – a style that befits the former lordly French owner who threw extravagant parties here to entertain royalty. There are sweeping staircases, vaulted ceilings, tromp l'oeil frescoes, fleets of salons and galleries, not to mention brocade-covered sofas, glittering chandeliers, marble statues and handsome oil paintings. Suites (nothing so dull as a bedroom) are sumptuous with dizzyingly high ceilings, oriental rugs on ancient terracotta floors, Renaissance-inspired furnishings and heavy fabrics. They are littered with paintings, marble busts, tapestries and rococo mirrors. Discreetly hidden is every hi-tech gadget a well-heeled traveller could want while the marbled bathrooms pamper with Bulgari products. You'll want to recover on one of the tiger-striped chairs in the private art gallery, among the palm trees in the courtyard, or on the rooftop terrace with the domes and towers of Florence at your feet.

Love time	Bed down in a suite whose walls and ceiling are a froth of frescoes.
Love bites	How about dinner on the rooftop terrace, served by your private butler?
Love it up	Sample some retail culture in the designer shops of Via Tornabuoni, then soak up the real thing in the Uffizi Gallery's 45 rooms of art treasures.

Bellissimo! Live like a Florentine aristocrat.

Casa Howard
Via Della Scala 18
00187 Florence
T +39 0669 924 555
F +39 0667 94644
E info@casahoward.it
W casahoward-florence.com
Jenifer Howard Forneris
11 rooms
Rates €160-260, breakfast €15

Airport   Florence (4 km)
                Pisa (80 km)

Arrival   From main rail station: go
                to the Piazza Santa Maria
                Novella, turn right into the
                Via della Scala and Casa
                Howard is on your right.

Open all year round

Casa Howard

B&B is far too pedestrian a term to describe this 12-room extravaganza in an old palazzo just yards from Piazza Santa Maria Novella. As the latest creation of owners Count Leonardi and Jenifer Howard Forneris it joins their original Rome success story. That means burying blandness and uniformity in favour of original and imaginatively themed rooms. Twin this with all the warmth of a private home plus can't-do-enough service and you're in clover. Ancient features are axiomatic in Florence and there's no cheating here; parquet and stone floors, heavy wood doors, marble chimney pieces and numerous fine artworks. However it's the stunning decor and host of luxurious little extras that turn a stay here into a treat. We were hard pushed to decide between the extravagant Drawing room in soigné black; the lavish Oriental room with its emperor-sized bed and erotic prints or the impressively tome-lined Library. Smokers should head for the Camel room (very droll!). There's even a Turkish bath – exclusively yours when staying in the Garden room. Housekeepers, aka 'house genies,' are also trained to add to Casa Howard's spell.

Love time   We were gladly bidden to the Hidden room, where bold crimson decor provides a backdrop to a gigantic capitonne bedhead and sunken bath.

Love bites   Breakfast is delicious freshly baked pastries delivered to your room.

Love it up   Check out Jenifer Howard's hitlist of places you might otherwise miss.

Bellissimo! ▶   Where Florence lays on the fabulous.

Hotel Casci
Via Cavour 13
50129 Florence
T +39 055 211 686
F +39 055 239 6461
E info@hotelcasci.com
W hotelcasci.com
Armando and Carla Lombardi
24 rooms
Rates €90-150

Closed second half of January

Extras   Courtesy of
Room for Romance:
Honeymooners receive a
complimentary bottle of
champagne.

Airport   Florence (4 km)
Pisa (80 km)

Arrival   From the Duomo: turn
north into Via Martelli,
which becomes Via
Cavour. The hotel is on
the left.

Hotel Casci

The general consensus among former guests at this small, right-in-the-thick-of-things hotel occupying the second floor of a 15th century palazzo is "the Lombardis make it". Praise is lavished on father Armando, mother Carla and son Paolo, who go the extra mile to ensure guests have a good time. The Casci may be straightforwardly done up but it doesn't eschew style. The building previously enjoyed aristocratic connections with the powerful Medicis (look out for the coat of arms above the entrance), and was briefly the home of famous composer Gioacchino Rossini. Rooms – some with balcony or original stone columns – are simple but spotless, with tall shuttered windows, two-tone walls and cheerful bedspreads. Breakfast is taken in the frescoed dining room, with its chequered marble floor. But back to the solicitous Lombardis, who are forever bustling about. Stay for three nights or more in February or November and they'll even give you a complimentary museum pass. Rossini would probably call that going out on a high note.

Love time   Book a quiet room at the rear with views over courtyard and magnolia trees.
Love bites It's the lounge bar for frothy cappuccinos, the frescoed dining room for breakfast, and several restaurants right outside for the rest.
Love it up It's all walkable: you're just around the corner from the Palazzo Medici, the Duomo and the Galleria dell'Accademia.

Bellissimo!   Florentine friendliness on a budget.

Gallery Hotel Art
Vicolo dell'Oro 5
50123 Florence
T +39 0552 7263
F +39 0552 68557
E gallery@lungarnohotels.com
W lungarnohotels.com
Alessio Ianna
74 rooms
Rates €260-1,188
Dinner from €110

Open all year round

Extras

Airport

Arrival

Courtesy of
Room for Romance:
Room upgrade subject
to availability, plus a bottle
of prosecco.

Florence (10 km)
Pisa (81 km)

From the Ponte Vecchio:
walk via Lungarno degli
Acciaiuoli, then take a
right and left. The hotel is
1 km from Santa Maria
Novella rail station.

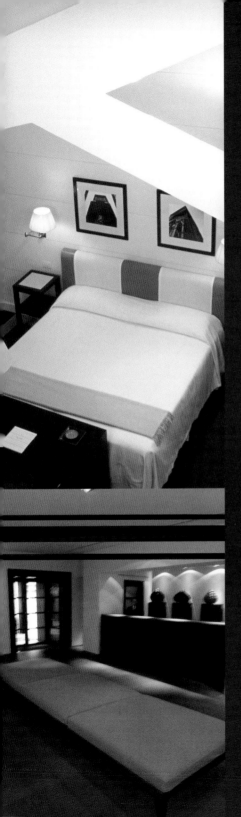

Gallery Hotel Art

This is the perfect foil to a city laden with classical history. Florence's first contemporary boutique hotel marries minimalist chic and cutting-edge design with shades of Japan. The city that invented the Renaissance has been given a makeover here, with bold modern art and contemporary furniture in browns, beiges and ochres complementing chic black-and-white photography. The reading room lounge has a large library, with art books and magazines lining the shelves next to modern objets d'art, and there's a rooftop terrace bar for warm summer evenings. Leather headboards, huge mirrors and simple but beautifully framed architectural photos on walls add texture to the rooms. The river Arno (and the Ponte Vecchio) are only a few minutes away, and all eight penthouse suites look out across a vista of terracotta rooftops. The hip and sexy Fusion Bar has become one of *the* places in town, so we happily sipped a cocktail there and dipped into the innovative Japanese menu. Cool, contemporary and right in the heart of things – this is a place to be seen.

Love time	Splurge on the Penthouse Palazzo Vecchio, with its rooftop terrace.
Love bites	Nibble on some sushi (room service delivers this and de-lish Italian snacks).
Love it up	Where to start? Take in the Galleria dell'Accademia (for Michelangelo's David), the gothic Santa Maria Novella and the Ponte Vecchio.
Bellissimo!	Sleek modern quarters in a city bursting with history.

Hotel Loggiato dei Serviti
Piazza SS Annunziata 3
50122 Florence
T +39 055 289 592
F +39 055 289 595
E info@loggiatodeiservitihotel.it
W loggiatodeiservitihotel.it
Rodolfo Budini Gattai
38 Rooms
Rates €154-205

Open all year round

Extras

Courtesy of
Room for Romance:
A complimentary chilled
bottle of champagne in
your room.

Airport

Florence (10 km)
Pisa (85 km)

Arrival

From the Duomo: take
Via Cavour to Piazza San
Marco, then Via Battisti.
The hotel is 600m from
Santa Maria Novella rail
station.

Loggiato dei Serviti

This 16th century Renaissance palazzo on the Piazza Annunziata once gave hospitality to religious prelates passing through Florence. Nowadays it welcomes those of a more hedonistic persuasion and has been skillfully converted while retaining its many original features. Lofty ceilings, glittering chandeliers, tiled and stripped wooden floors scattered with jewel-coloured rugs are the hallmarks of this stylish boutique hotel. Shades of cream and cappuccino are counterpointed by vibrant fabrics, Florentine decorative touches and antiques. Architectural prints line the bar and the spacious sitting areas are an invitation to lounge. Bursting with antiques and piled with fluffy pillows, each of the distinctive bedrooms has its own story to tell. Frescoes, canopied and four-poster beds (one reputedly belonged to Napoleon III's mistress), hand-painted furnishings and high ceilings lift the spirits. Early-to-bedders should snuggle down in a room at the back, while those into people-watching can soak up all the colour of the square below – one of Florence's loveliest – from their front-facing balcony. Charming staff can't do enough to help.

Love time	For contemporary cool we'd dive into the mansard-roofed Room 39.
Love bites	You're spoilt for choice with an array of places to dine out just steps away.
Love it up	Florence awaits: don't miss Michelangelo's David, the Ponte Vecchio and the Uffizi. There's retail therapy, too, in scores of leather accessory shops.

Bellissimo! Elegant old-world charm in stylish Renaissance conversion.

Palazzo Niccolini al Duomo
Via dei Servi 2
50122 Florence
T +39 0552 82412
F +39 0552 90979
E info@niccolinidomepalace.com
W niccolinidomepalace.com
Maura Pedroni
10 rooms
Rates €270
Dinner from €70

Open all year round

Extras   Courtesy of
Room for Romance:
A complimentary bottle of
wine and if possible, a
room upgrade.

Airport   Florence (4 km)
Pisa (80 km)

Arrival   The hotel is 600m from
Santa Maria Novella rail
station. From the Duomo:
go north along Via dei
Servi, and the hotel is on
your right.

Palazzo Niccolini al Duomo

This stunning private palazzo dating back to the 15th century is bang in the heart of historic Florence, just yards from the Duomo. A one-time studio for the sculptor Donatello, the residence was handed down through generations of the aristocratic Naldini family before passing to its present owners Filippo and Ginevra Niccolini. Recent renovations have retained all its patina of lineage and time, while adding essential modern comforts. Now you too can live like an aristocrat in ducal surrounds in this decidedly swish Florentine B&B. Take time to admire the awesomely grand salons with their high painted ceilings and flamboyant Renaissance style wall frescoes, imposing marble fireplaces, fine antiques and ornately carved panelling. Generously proportioned suites, all lavishly decorated and with every comfort, have benefited from the same careful TLC. The Niccolinis share their home happily and hospitably with their guests. Its discreet location behind a pair of imposing gates adds to its noble allure.

Love time	Go the full Duomo… in the penthouse Duomo suite with its own jacuzzi and knockout views of its namesake.
Love bites	Breakfast in the drawing room; good restos and bars are steps away.
Love it up	You're right where the action is: minutes from the Ponte Vecchio, the Uffizi and some terrific shops.

Bellissimo! Stylish ducal domain right by the Duomo.

Hotel Santa Maria Novella
Piazza Santa Maria Novella 1
50100 Florence
T +39 0552 71841
F +39 0552 718 4199
E info@hotelsantamarianovella.it
W hotelsantamarianovella.it
Claudio Delli
44 rooms
Rates €190-450

Open all year round

Extras

Courtesy of
Room for Romance:
A bottle of prosecco for
guests booking Bellavista
suite. Upgrade to superior
class room when possible.

Airport

Florence (5 km)
Pisa (85 km)

Arrival

The hotel is 100m from
Santa Maria Novella rail
station. Turn left at station
and walk past Santa
Maria Novella church.

Santa Maria Novella

Angels guard the foyer, cherubs cavort on gilded ceilings and inlaid marble gleams beneath your feet as you enter this stately 19th century Florentine hotel, wonderfully restored to its former glory by architect Marianna Gagliardi. Wood-panelled walls in soft turquoises, creams and greys add a touch of grace to the sitting room – where you can lounge in front of a marble fireplace with the day's newspaper – and the Napoleon room, hung with Napoleonic paintings and etchings. Dove-grey pastels add an air of cool elegance to the formal dining room while the classical bar is a real window on Florence, with brilliant views of the ochre and white chequered facade of Basilica Santa Maria Novella, on the piazza of the same name. Heavy swagged curtains, canopied beds and luscious antiques create period bedrooms worthy of Byron, counterpointed by sleek flat-screen TVs and internet points. Each room is different, while some have a view from the skylight above the marble baths. You can gaze at the soaring basilica while breakfasting on coffee and fresh *cornetti* before hitting the big sights.

Love time	Lie back and gaze up at the floodlit Duomo from the Bellavista suite.
Love bites	Take your pick from dozens of restaurants within easy reach.
Love it up	You're just 200m from the Duomo. Ready to spend? Take your credit card for an outing along shopping street extraordinaire, Via Tornabuoni.

Bellissimo! Nineteenth century splendour and a room with a view.

Torre di Bellosguardo
Via Roti Michelozzi 2
50124 Florence
T +39 0552 298 145
F +39 0552 29008
E info@torrebellosguardo.com
W torrebellosguardo.com
Amerigo Franchetti
16 rooms
Rates €290-390

Extras

Courtesy of
Room for Romance:
A welcome drink on
arrival.

Airport
Florence (8 km)
Pisa (80 km)

Arrival
From A1 motorway: exit
at Firenze Certosa and
follow signs for Porta
Romana. The hotel is a
five-minute drive from
city centre.

Open all year round

Torre di Bellosguardo

Set in the hills above Florence, narrow lanes curve up through olive groves to an avenue of cypresses framing this spectacular tower. Built in the 13th century as a hunting lodge, it later became an impressive Renaissance villa. Enter the vast entrance hall – the former ballroom – and you may want to throw caution to the wind with a cha-cha under the soaring frescoed ceiling. An elegant little wood-panelled bar lifts your spirits even higher. The historic rooms downstairs are the perfect spot to lose yourself in and upstairs, each bedroom holds a surprise. A 16th century rosette-studded ceiling here, warm wooden beams there, or a gilded antique four-poster in which to play. Some have dreamy views over the city, others of the Tuscan hills. Outside, terraces tumble down towards Florence, old-fashioned roses smother pergolas and lotus plants bloom in ponds. Wide green lawns frame the turquoise pool, while at night the garden glints with fireflies and Moroccan lanterns twinkle. A kitchen garden keeps the dining room stocked with freshest produce and there's a menagerie of ducks, rabbits, chickens and a Shetland pony (a local Casanova, it would seem) and even a resident parrot. The new spa is made for pampering.

Love time	Take Suite 11, with its four-poster bed; the ultimate room with a view.
Love bites	Breakfast on produce freshly plucked from the orchard in summer.
Love it up	Feast on the vista of Florence's rose-coloured roofs spread at your feet.

Bellissimo! Dreamy hideaway for lotus eaters.

Relais Santa Croce
Via Ghibellina 87
50122 Florence
T +39 055 234 2230
F +39 055 234 1195
E info@relaisantacroce.com
W relaisantacroce.com
Marika Caliolo
24 rooms
Rates €350-1,800
Dinner from €140

Open all year round

Extras

Courtesy of
Room for Romance:
Breakfast in bed and
flowers in your room.

Airport

Florence (6 km)
Pisa (80 km)

Arrival

By car: the hotel is
reached via Corso dei
Tintori and Piazza Santa
Croce. Parking available
at €30 day. By train: Santa
Maria Novella rail station
is ten minutes away.

Relais Santa Croce

Guests rave about Relais Santa Croce. This newly restored five-star palazzo within a stone's throw of the Duomo is attracting plaudits faster than reviewers can reach for their pens. An impeccably restored 17th century villa, it was once the magnificent quarters of the Pope's treasurer, complete with imposing granite columns. Masterful restoration has returned the Palazzo Ciofi-Jacometti to its original splendour, retaining the building's fabulous architectural detailing and 300-year-old frescoes. Not that the owners have tried to recreate a period timepiece: instead, contemporary furnishings blend with the building's original historic fabric to striking effect. The result is a supremely stylish residence that breathes elegance. Soft uplighters glow against the ornate boiserie panels and soaring ceiling of the lounge, while the adjacent music room has a small stage used for musical soirées. Bedrooms spring a few surprises, with the accent on chic shades of chestnut, stone and russet. Mounds of outsize pillows, gleaming marble bathrooms and attentive staff add to the blissfully cosseted feel.

Love time   For utter indulgence, take one of the two Royal suites: you'll have a huge bed, a steam shower and a vast jacuzzi tub to play in.

Love bites   Enjoy deliciously simple Tuscan fare in the intimate, candlelit restaurant.

Love it up   The art treasures of the Bargello and the Uffizi are all within easy reach.

Bellissimo!   Florentine relais with rave reviews.

Hotel Savoy
Piazza della Repubblica 7
50123 Florence
T +39 0552 7351
F +39 0552 735 888
E reservations@hotelsavoy.it
W roccofortehotels.com
Davide Bertilaccio
88 rooms, 14 suites
Rates €470–2,100
Dinner from €100

Airport   Florence (5 km)
Pisa (80 km)

Arrival   The hotel is in the city
centre between the
Duomo and the Ponte
Vecchio. It is a few
minutes walk from Santa
Maria Novella rail station.

Open all year round

The Savoy

The classic, turn-of-the-century facade gives little away – yet step inside and you glide into spaces of sleek minimalism and fresh modernity. Colours are cool and neutral, ceilings lofty, floors a swathe of limestone or pale parquet. Elegant Milanese sofas mix with funky furnishings – perhaps a zebra striped cushion or huge painting of fashion shoes. It's stylish, sharp and contemporary. After a hard day's shopping and sightseeing, the bedrooms, with their muted shades and modish photography, offer just the right smooth and soothing surroundings. Bathrooms mix marble decadence – you'll never want to get out of the bathtubs – with the glitter of mosaics and fabulous potions. If you can't get a room on the fifth floor, with its rooftop views, book one overlooking the Piazza della Repubblica. Darlings, this is the heart of the city. While staff unpack your cases and press your designer togs, you can be drinking in the city's cultural hotspots – or maybe a Martini in the hotel's swish bar L'Incontro. The best selection in Florence, naturally.

Love time	Push the boat out and book a suite. Acres of space, Bang & Olufsen sound systems, fabulous views; some even have have private steam rooms.
Love bites	Food fresh from the Florentine markets is turned into modern Tuscan cooking in the elegant surroundings of L'Incontro restaurant.
Love it up	The panoramic rooftop gym might just persuade you to work up a sweat.
Bellissimo!	Designer luxury in a Renaissance city.

Villa La Massa
Via della Massa 24
50012 Florence - Candeli
T +39 055 62611
F +39 055 633 102
E info@villalamassa.it
W villalamassa.it
Francesca Tozzi
27 rooms, 10 suites
Rates €380-470
Dinner from €160

Open April – October

Extras
Courtesy of
Room for Romance:
Choice of strawberries
with champagne, fruit
hamper or cantucci
biscuits with Vin Santo.
Upgrade if possible.

Airport
Florence (15 km)
Pisa (90 km)

Arrival
From A1: exit Firenze Sud
then Bagno a Ripoli –
Pontassieve; left at Candeli
lights. Rail station 10 km.

Villa La Massa

This sumptuous 16th century Medici villa hugging the banks of the River Arno and set against the Tuscan hills has hosted a roll-call of vintage Hollywood names over the years. Clark Gable, Liz Taylor and David Niven bedded down here, while David Bowie and Iman tied the knot in its beautiful private chapel. Just a few miles from Florence – so you can kiss the tourist crowds goodbye – Villa La Massa is a place to luxuriate. Lustrous rooms glowing in vibrant colours are spread among the hotel's three villas, some with four-posters and all with river or garden views. Finely crafted details are everywhere: fabrics woven in traditional Florentine mills, hand-made furniture, expensive Carrara marble bathrooms with deep tubs. The terrace of the hotel's Il Verrocchio restaurant, with the water rippling just below, was made for smoochily candlelit dinners. Chef Andrea Quagliarella's menus embrace the best of Tuscan and Mediterranean cooking. Stroll among vines, peach trees and olive groves in the riverbank gardens, cosset yourself with indulgent treatments in the beauty farm or sample some of the cellar's 400-odd labels.

Love time	Gaze at sunsets over the river from the glass-walled top Junior suites.
Love bites	Mouthwatering signature dishes include fillet of beef with Chianti and truffles, cuttlefish with black olives and Zuccotto fiorentina – dessert to die for.
Love it up	Play tennis, jog and work out, or buzz into Florence on the free shuttle.
Bellissimo!	Swish Renaissance villa in delectable river setting.

Villa San Michele
Via Doccia 4, Fiesole
50014 Florence
T +39 055 567 8200
F +39 055 567 8250
E reservations@villasanmichele.net
W villasanmichele.com
Maurizio Saccani
21 rooms, 25 suites
Rates €909-1,084, suites €1,309-2,244
Dinner from €200

Closed 20 Nov – 23 March

Extras   Courtesy of
Room for Romance;
A complimentary chilled
bottle of sparkling wine in
your room.

Airport Florence (10 km)
Pisa (90 km)

Arrival From A1 motorway: take
exit marked Firenze Sud.
The hotel is 8 km from
here. By train: 15 minutes
from Santa Maria Novella
rail station.

Villa San Michele

Check in here and swoon. This spectacularly sited former monastery is unquestionably one of Italy's finest hotels, with a celebrity guest list to prove it. Sprawling in wooded grounds in the hilltop village of Fiesole, Villa San Michele was a place of prayer and abstinence back in the 15th century. Napoleon later bagged it for his HQ, and today's classically beautiful hotel – awesomely restored and loaded with original features – is fit for an emperor. How those friars missed out: Italianate bedrooms now come with canopied and wrought-iron beds, elegant antiques and opulent bathrooms stocked with Bulgari lotions, while suites have private gardens and stunning views of Florence. Antique furnished salons are hung with works of art while the former chapel is now a grand reception hall. The loggia is a stunning setting for evening *aperitivi*, with the jewelled lights of Florence spread at your feet. Step outside the wisteria-clad walls and wander among orange and lemon trees in fragrant wooded grounds.

Love time	Lap up the views from the Old Chapel, romantically hidden in the gardens.
Love bites	Gaze at restored frescoes of the Last Supper in the Cenacolo restaurant while feasting on chef Attilo di Fabrizio's brilliant Tuscan fare.
Love it up	Take the shuttle into Florence, pedal around the village of Fiesole or sign up for cookery classes; some of Europe's top chefs come here to teach.
Bellissimo!	Much-lauded celebrity haunt on Florentine hilltop.

Villa Mangiacane
Via Faltignano 4
San Casciano, 50026 Florence
T +39 055 829 0123
F +39 055 829 0358
E info@mangiacane.it
W mangiacane.com
Paolo Barzagli
8 suites
Rates €300-2,500
Dinner from €140

Open all year round

Extras   Courtesy of
Room for Romance:
A bottle of prosecco,
fresh flowers and a
romantic after-dinner bath.

Airport   Florence (15 km)
Pisa (90 km)

Arrival   From Florence: take A1
south, then SS2 towards
Tavarnuzze. Turn right
towards San Andrea in
Percussina, and hotel is
on the right after village.

142

Villa Mangiacane

Glass of wine in hand, stand beneath magnificent 15th century frescoes and gaze over your private Tuscan vineyard to the distinctive skyline of Florence. Welcome to Villa Mangiacane, once home of the powerful Macchiavelli family and now a sybaritic retreat that mixes Italian antiques, Renaissance frescoes and modern art with some decadent living. Wander through ground floor salons, the library and wine cellar; relax on a boldly striped sofa on the loggia; sip a prosecco in the sculpture garden; doze over a book beside the pool. Bedrooms – none less than a suite – have a restrained opulence with crisp, clean colours, generous fabrics, rugs on polished floors and breathtaking views. Grand antiques – perhaps a carved four-poster or an elegant chaise longue – mix with contemporary paintings. Bathrooms are cool, marbled and sleek with a hint of gracious Art Deco. At night, after dining in the chandeliered and mirrored dining room, you'll be drawn to the frescoed loggia – perfumed with flowers and lit with soft candles – and the dreamy views of distant Florence. Just the two of you and the twinkling Tuscan hills.

Love time	We adored our suite with a mezzanine bedroom – an extra level of pleasure, should you need it.
Love bites	Dine on the terrace, in the atmospheric cellars or around the fire in winter.
Love it up	Flex your plastic with a personally guided tour of Florence's designer shops.
Bellissimo!	Rich Renaissance hideaway for pleasure seekers.

Fattoria Borghetto di Chiena
Località Pieve a Pitiana
50066 Donnini Reggello
T +39 055 860 5550
F +39 055 860 336
E info@borghettodichiena.it
W borghettodichiena.it
Nerina Keeley
18 rooms
Rates €350-450
Dinner from €90

Closed January

Extras Courtesy of
Room for Romance:
A vineyard picnic with
prosecco and tasters of
Tuscan specialities.
Special honeymoon rates.

Airport Florence (35 km)

Arrival From Florence: take A1
towards Arezzo then S69
towards Pontassieve. At
Leccio turn right towards
Reggello. Hotel is signed
on the right.

Borghetto di Chiena

We discovered Borghetto di Chiena – a wonderful old farmhouse dating back to the 11th century – just before its doors were due to open as a luxury country house hotel. Set in a private estate on the doorstep of Reggello – a glorious Tuscan hilltop town with views over the Chianti hills – it sits amid its own vineyards and olive groves beside the Arno valley. Just out of wrappers, this is clearly destined to be a very special place. The 18 spacious suites – some with their own secluded garden – are pure romantic-rustic, with stone archways, fireplaces and wrought-iron four-posters wrapped in silk drapes, matched by antique furniture and gorgeous, richly coloured fabrics. All have stunning 360 degree terraces with vineyard views and outsize jacuzzi tubs for two. This is also the place for wine buffs: you'll have the chance to quaff, compare and take home wines from numerous regional growers as well as – from 2007 – those from the hotel's own estate. There's a magnificent vaulted dining room, a private pool in the grounds, terrific views, and Tuscany's art treasure towns within close reach.

Love time   Terraced rooms with every comfort look over a timeless Tuscan landscape.
Love bites   Expect the best of seasonal Tuscan fare: pasta with wild hare sauce, freshly baked breads with artichoke tapenade, porcini mushrooms.
Love it up   Gucci and Prada fans can stock up at the fashion designers' outlet close by.

Bellissimo!   Country farmhouse with stellar cellars in quintessential Tuscany.

Villa I Bossi
Gragnone 44-46
52100 Arezzo
T +39 0575 365 642
F +39 0575 964 900
E franvig@ats.it
W villaibossi.com
Francesca Viguali Albergotti
11 rooms
Rates €125-145
Dinner from €25

Open all year round

Extras

Courtesy of
Room for Romance:
A complimentary bottle
of wine in your room.
Upgraded room for
honeymooners.

Airport   Florence (60 km)

Arrival   From Florence: A1 to
Arezzo exit. Follow signs
for Stadio then Bagnoro-
Gragnone. Hotel is approx
4 km from the stadium just
after the Gragnone sign.

Villa I Bossi

Ensconce yourselves at this splendid 14th century *villa nobiliare* (I Bossi takes its name from the serried ranks of box trees in the surrounding Italianate gardens) and chances are the owner, the Marchesa Albergotti, will offer you the grand tour (it's been her husband's family seat since 1320). Francesca, as she's known, will charmingly direct guests across stone-floored rooms decorated with mellow frescoes and fine pieces, including furniture seized by ancestors in the Napoleonic Wars. She'll take you down into cellars where there's an 18th century weighbridge and other curious items, and draw your attention to the family's private sacristy with its serenely beautiful relics. Look out for the gargantuan 15th century chimneypiece in the library, and perhaps opt for the room whose ensuite bath is carved out of a single block of stone. Francesca also teaches cookery and so enthuses guests that they often end up as students. An outbuilding has been converted into additional rooms in the old lemon groves. Here, there or indeed anywhere on the estate provides a perfect excuse to quaff the family's own Chianti. Blissy Bossi, no less.

Love time   Perchance to dream… from antique ironwork bedsteads with floaty fabrics.
Love bites   Breakfast on local specialities in the atmospheric old kitchen, whose huge
                  fireplace and walls are bedecked with shiny copper pans.
Love it up   Try visiting Arezzo, famed for its exquisite della Francesca frescoes.

Bellissimo!   Ancient Tuscan where-it's-at hosted by aristocrat.

Relais San Pietro in Polvano
Località Polvano 3
52043 Castiglion Fiorentino
T +39 0575 650 100
F +39 0575 650 255
E info@polvano.com
W polvano.com
Luigi Protti
10 rooms
Rates €180-300
Dinner from €60

Closed November – March

Extras

Courtesy of
Room for Romance:
A complimentary aperitif
with your evening
meal.

Airport

Florence (100 km)
Pisa (140 km)

Arrival

From Florence: take the
A1 south, exit at Monte
San Savino, follow
directions for Castiglion
Fiorentino, then follow
signs for Polvano.

Relais San Pietro in Polvano

Love is evident in every stone of this 300-year-old farmhouse, carefully restored and run with a passion for perfection by the gently hospitable Protti family. Solid country furniture, kilims and cream furnishings with modern touches work well with the building's bricked archways, terracotta floors and heavy beamed ceilings. Feel big-city stress melt away as you make yourself at home in the calming white-walled bedrooms with their wrought-iron beds, white bedspreads, oriental rugs and wooden painted furniture. On winter nights, cosy up near a log fire; on long summer days, feast on the views from the open terrace and wonderfully private pool. Renaissance artists could not have painted a more idyllic scene than the rolling Tuscan hills dotted with medieval villages, olive groves and pencil-sharp cypress trees that surround the tiny hamlet of Polvano, snuggled between Arezzo and Cortona. With a ban on TVs, smoking and under-12s, this is a place designed to soothe the soul. It's also tailor-made for honeymoons – before or after the wedding!

Love time	The almost monastic simplicity of the bedrooms simply begs you to sin.
Love bites	Freshly baked bread and green-gold olive oil from the Relais' own olive groves are the start of mouthwatering dinners of traditional Tuscan food, served in the fetching former stables or on the terrace.
Love it up	Walk, ride, play tennis. It's also a great base for exploring historic Tuscany.
Bellissimo! ▶	Dreamily romantic gem bedded in the Tuscan hills.

Hotel Villa Marsili
Viale C. Battisti 13
52044 Cortona
T +39 0575 605 252
F +39 0575 605 618
E info@villamarsili.net
W villamarsili.net
Stefano Meacci
27 rooms
Rates €132-310
Dinner from €58

Closed late Jan – Feb

Extras   Courtesy of
Room for Romance:
A bottle of prosecco in
your room and an
afternoon aperitif.

Airport   Florence (120 km)
Pisa (190 km)

Arrival   From Florence: take the
A1 towards Rome and
exit at Valdichiana.
Take the E45 Siena-
Perugia road and exit at
Cortona.

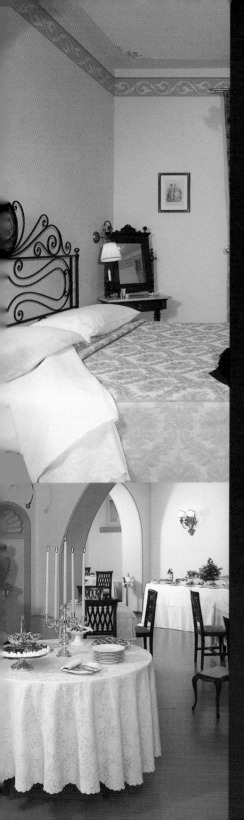

Villa Marsili

Drink in the views of the Tuscan hills as you sit on the terrace and sip your complimentary sundowner, reflecting on six centuries of history. Brilliantly located within the ancient city walls of the stunning Etruscan and medieval hill town of Cortona, Villa Marsili began life as a 14th century church – Chiesa della Madonna degli Alemanni. Home to a miraculous statue of the Virgin, it was converted into a patrician palazzo in 1786. It still feels more like a private residence than a hotel, with many of its finest features recently restored after centuries of neglect. A series of arches lead you through the airy public areas with their cool Tuscan terracotta-tiled floors. Bedrooms glow in burnished shades of red and gold, with many having hand-painted furniture. Park up the car and take to your feet; the hotel is within walking distance of all Cortona's main sights. Back in your boudoir, consider carefully the romantic possibilities presented by a wrought-iron bedstead, a hydro-massage bath and a Murano glass chandelier. If you're short of ideas, golf, tennis, swimming, cycling and riding are all on offer locally.

Love time   Passionate reds and golds and a round jacuzzi bath set the mood
               for love in Suite 20.

Love bites   Breakfast on home-made Tuscan fare beneath a pergola in the garden.

Love it up   After a hard day's history, chill on the terrace with a complimentary aperitif.

Bellissimo!   The steeples and towers of medieval Cortona are right on your doorstep.

Villa Poggiano
Via di Poggiano 7
53045 Montepulciano
T +39 0578 75 8292
F +39 0578 71 5635
E info@villapoggiano.com
W villapoggiano.com
Stefania Savini
9 rooms
Rates €190-210, suites €230-300

Airports   Perugia (60 km)
Florence (100 km)
Pisa (150 km)

Arrival   From Montepulciano: take
the S146 towards Pienza.
About 2 km along this
road turn left, following
signs to the hotel.

Open March – November

Villa Poggiano

Water babies will love Villa Poggiano. With good reason – the pool is fit for an emperor to make a splash. No ordinary pool this, but one that's been magnificently marbled, around which a number of striking neo-classical statues and graceful figures from ancient times stare enviously down. Having said that, we think you'll be just as easily struck by the villa's other virtues. Such as its aspect on a hilltop set in 15 acres of parkland with lofty cypress trees and great views of the Orcia Valley. It demands you settle down and share it with a bottle or three of renowned local vino from nearby Montepulciano and Monticchiello. First built in the 17th century, it has been remodelled over the years and today's owners, the Savinis, have overlaid it with the sheen that comes from genuinely committed family management. The sitting room has a vast and prepossessing fireplace, lit on cooler evenings, while tables are elegantly laid with flowers in the pretty dining room. The atmosphere, whatever the weather, remains typically Tuscan-warm.

Love time   Slumber in the villa itself or gaze on olive groves from the adjacent lodge.
Love bites   Start the day with crumbly pastries and frothy cappuccinos.....yum.
Love it up   Uncover fascinating old towns such as Montalcino (home of Brunello wine)
                  and Pienza, famous for its ancient sulphur baths. Sooner chill? Indulge in
                  an in-room beauty treatment.

Bellissimo! ▶   The place to be in pool position.

Relais San Bruno
Via di Pescaia 5/7
53045 Montepulciano
T +39 0578 716 222
F +39 0578 715 084
E info@sanbrunorelais.com
W sanbrunorelais.it
Alberto Pavoncelli
6 rooms, 1 apartment
Rates €250-300

Closed mid Nov – March

Extras

Courtesy of
Room for Romance:
A bottle of fine
Montepulciano wine in
your room.

Airport

Florence (112 km)
Pisa (152 km)

Arrival

From Florence: take
the S2 south. After San
Quirico d'Orcia turn left
and take the S146
towards Montepulciano.

Relais San Bruno

Think Tuscany, think olive greens and terracotta reds, think hilltop towns and rolling vineyards, think Montepulciano. What better place to stay than the highest of Tuscan hill towns; gorgeous views and gorgeous wines, too. Relais San Bruno is tucked below the walls of this Renaissance hilltop town, wrapped in green meadows and overlooking the Basilica of San Biagio – a stunning location away from the crowds. The dusky pink, stone villa with its pantile roof and wooden shutters is a cosy but stylish retreat; just six rooms, each with its own entrance. Sunny colours, terracotta floors, white sofas, elegant wooden furnishings and soft lighting create a calm, understatedly elegant air. Pure linen on the beds, jacuzzis in the bathroom, bowls of fruit and flowers add discreet luxury touches. There are shady corners in the garden, a hammock slung between trees and a secluded swimming pool with wide open views of the Tuscan countryside. Pretty walks in the Parco della Val d'Orcia start almost from the villa's front door – though with drinks and nibbles brought to you at the pool, we were tempted to just stay put.

Love time	Escape to Snow White's House, a tiny cottage wrapped in rose trees.
Love bites	Delicious breakfasts – organic home-made breads, cakes and pastries – can be eaten al fresco in the garden or orangery.
Love it up	Private vineyard tours and wine tastings? Yes, please.

Bellissimo! Your own private villa – almost.

Castello di Vicarello
58044 Poggi del Sasso
Cinigiano
T/F +39 0564 990 718
E info@vicarello.it
W castellodivicarello.it
Carlo Baccheschi Barti
4 suites, 1 villa
Rates €270-550

Open all year round

Extras Courtesy of
Room for Romance:
A complimentary chilled
bottle of champagne in
your room.

Airport Florence (100 km)
Pisa (140 km)

Arrival From Siena: take the
E78/S223 to Paganico,
then Sasso d'Ombrone.
Take Via Vicarello on right,
go left at fork after 700m.
3.5 km further.

Castello di Vicarello

Far away from the well-trodden Chiantishire trail stands a 12th century castle set among olive groves and vineyards. Aurora and Carlo Baccheschi have transformed this once-abandoned ruin into a brilliantly chic hideaway. Italian and oriental styles have been skillfully mixed here, with Indonesian furniture and antiques counterpointed by bright splashes of contemporary art. The four suites and a villa are finished to the highest standard and each has its own highly individual appeal. Colour-washed walls are offset by rustic stone, gleaming stripped wooden floors, venetian blinds and mellowed flagstones. Tactile leather, rustic rattan, intricately carved wooden bedheads, real working fireplaces and big bathrooms make this a castle dedicated to aesthetic pleasures. Sip a glass or two of chilled vino bianco as you float languidly in the infinity pool carved from travertine rock, where lofty cypress trees stand sentinel. The 60 acres of grounds contain a vineyard and over a thousand olive trees, not to mention fruit orchards ripening under the Tuscan sun.

Love time   The Sassi suite is a window on nature, while the Giardino Segreto has a deliciously private garden.

Love bites   Aurora's home-made soups and pigeon paté will perk up jaded palates.

Love it up   The best of Tuscany is at your door: try Siena and Montalcino for starters.

Bellissimo! ▶   Chic, intimate castle hangout.

Castello di Velona
Località Velona
53024 Montalcino
T +39 0577 800 101
F +39 0577 835 661
E info@castellodivelona.it
W castellodivelona.it
Alessandro Ercolane
2 rooms, 22 suites
Rates €210-650
Dinner from €80

Closed November – February

Extras

Courtesy of
Room for Romance:
A room upgrade
subject to availability.

Airport
Florence (120 km)
Pisa (160 km)

Arrival
Take the S2 south from
Florence, then follow
directions for Montalcino.
By train: go to
Buonconvento (12km).

Castello di Velona

Gaze from your window and you'll swear you're looking at a Renaissance painting. Tall poplar trees, dark olive groves, rolling vineyards and, in the distance, Tuscany's highest peak. This handsome medieval fortress turned villa is in a plum hilltop position overlooking the peaceful Val d'Orcia. Recently renovated, it combines all its ancient grandeur – oak-beamed ceilings, stone walls, mighty watchtower – with a light and elegant modern luxury; so smooth, you barely see the join. Richly coloured rugs sprawl on the terracotta floors, hand-painted trompe l'oeil borders decorate the stone walls, boldly striped sofas warm the vaulted spaces. Handsome double doors open into bedrooms of understated elegance. Colours are light and creamy with shots of blue, green and blood red adding a spicy tone. Polished antiques, embroidered bed linen and overflowing bowls of fruit add to the sense of warmth. Browse a book in the library, admire the frescoed chapel, sip a cocktail beside the pool or chill on the shady terrace drinking in those views.

Love time	Private balconies with views over Tuscany, marbled bathrooms with olive oil based potions. Why leave?
Love bites	Dine on top Tuscan cooking under the terrace's olive and cypress trees.
Love it up	Walk or cycle through Val d'Orcia from the hotel's doorstep, or go wine tasting – in nearby Montepulciano or in the hotel's own cellars.
Bellissimo!	Timeless Tuscany from a Renaissance retreat.

L'Andana
Località Badiola
58043 Castiglione della Pescaia
T +39 0564 944 800
F +39 0564 944 577
E info@andana.it
W andana.it
33 rooms
Rates €345-1,260
Dinner from €60

Closed February

Extras

Courtesy of
Room for Romance:
Bottle of Bollicine sparkling
wine. Special 'Under the
Tuscan Sun' offers.

Airport

Pisa (110 km)
Florence (120 km)

Arrival

From Florence: go south
to Grosseto, take the SP3
Castiglione road, and at
roundabout take second
right towards Castiglione
della Pescaia.

L'Andana

Take a glorious 500 acre estate stuffed with olive-clad hills and vineyards, and the former residence of the Grand Duke of Tuscany. Then rev up the neo-classical interiors with cool n' chic design by Ettore Mochetti, director of Architectural Digest Italy. Now stamp the cuisine with the imprint of Alain Ducasse, French masterchef extraordinaire. One treat comes overlaid with another at L'Andana. There's a traditional fattoria set around an interior courtyard, a magnificent new glasshouse-style foyer and bar, and some high-tech gadgetry in the rooms. Reception areas and suites have white-painted ceilings and walls, polished stone floors and drapey silk curtains setting off eye-catching sofas upholstered in lush silks; it's a look of artful simplicity. A restored granary houses the restaurant in a polished rustic environment. Diners catch sight of the kitchens where chefs trained by Ducasse rework classic Tuscan dishes. A pool, luxurious new spa (from April 2006) and a golf practice course complete the picture. Well, not quite: just beyond these fabulous surrounds you can glimpse the sea and the Isle of Giglio.

Love time   Suites entice with softly-softly beds, views and baths made for wallowing.
Love bites   Regional Tuscan cuisine majors on using ingredients from the estate; a seductive style created by Alain Ducasse, France's king of gastronomy.
Love it up   Enjoy spa pampering, take cookery lessons or scour Etruscan ruins.

Bellissimo!   Tuscan cool notched up with Ducasse class.

Pardini's Hermitage
Cala degli Alberi
Isola del Giglio
T +39 0564 809 034
F +39 0564 809 177
E info@hermit.it
W hermit.it
Federigo Pardini
13 rooms
Rates €230-370
Dinner included in room price

Airport   Pisa (140 km)
Rome Fiumicino (150 km)

Arrival   The island is reached by
ferry from Porto San
Stefano (reached via
S1/E80). Try to book
ahead and leave car at
San Stefano. Call hotel
to arrange launch transfer
on arrival.

Closed 15 Oct – end March

162

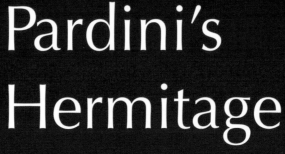

Pardini's Hermitage

Just you, your squeeze and the gin-clear Tyrrhenian Sea. No crowds, no traffic. Sounds just the ticket? Then check out Pardini's Hermitage, on Isola del Giglio – a cliffy island off the Tuscan coast that's a day-trip destination for most. A longer linger at this secluded retreat, accessible only by boat, is a perfect way to de-stress. Luggage is spirited away on a little motorised railway from Porto del Giglio, while arriving guests hop into the hotel's motorboat. Perched on top of a promontory overlooking a rugged bay, this family-run eyrie is far away from prying eyes. There are terraces for lounging, lunching and barbecueing under the pines, and plenty of hideaway corners for secret trysts. Compact bedrooms – some in the main house, others in the grounds – are simply furnished, with raftered ceilings, old stonework and terraces. Life at this 1950s built one-time family home is about chilling and enjoying the great outdoors. Savour the views with a glass of cold fizz, and maybe go the full skinny, dipping into clear waters from rocky coves.

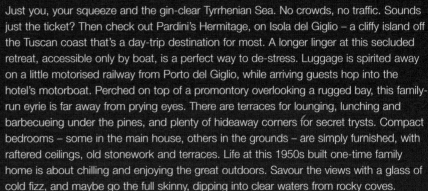

Love time	Enjoy a shiatsu massage or a meditation mattress with your soulmate.
Love bites	Tuck into wholesome, home-grown organic ingredients from the working farm (goats, pigs and sheep abound) and freshly caught fish.
Love it up	Discover teeming underwater life; saddle up a donkey for an island trek or treat yourself to some thalassotherapy (seawater) treatments.

Bellissimo! Away-from-it-all hermits never had it so good.

L'Olmo
Località Monticchiello
53020 Pienza
T +39 0578 755 133
F +39 0578 755 124
E info@olmopienza.it
W olmopienza.it
Francesca Lindo
1 room, 6 suites
Rates €170-290
Dinner from €110

Closed end Nov – Easter

Extras

Courtesy of
Room for Romance:
Welcome champagne
aperitif with pecorino
cheese. Room upgrade
if possible.

Airport

Florence (120 km)
Rome (190 km)

Arrival

From Florence: leave the
A1 south at Valdichiana.
From Rome: leave the A1
north at Chiusi-Chianciano
Terme. Train: Chiusi (30 km).

L'Olmo

If you're a sucker for sophisticated rusticity – and we are – then you'll love L'Olmo.
A 17th century Tuscan residence guarded by lofty cypress trees has been skillfully
transformed into an intimate locanda by owner Francesca Lindo. Picture two handsome
houses flanking a sheltered courtyard and a pretty garden, filled with local artefacts and
flowers tumbling from urns. Then there's an inviting pool area with loll-around loungers
and stunning views guaranteed to stop you in your tracks. L'Olmo straddles a plateau
and is surrounded by acres of wheatfields ruffled in the breeze with forested hills rolling
into the distance. Francesca supervises the kitchen; her seductive culinary offerings are
a great match for the famous local vino. Suites boasts a distinct design but share a
common theme of gleaming terracotta floors, polished antiques, Laura Ashley fabrics
and wood-beamed ceilings. Enjoy lazy poolside life, sink into comfy four-poster or
canopied beds, and soak in bathrooms tiled with local stone. Life can't be bad.

Love time	Choose an ultra-private suite with whirlpool and garden. One has a sunken living room and floor-to-ceiling glass wall overlooking those wheatfields.
Love bites	*Tipiche del territoria* recipes might include hand-made pasta followed by game or rabbit with olives. Tastes even better eaten under the stars.
Love it up	Check out Montalcino's vineyards or Bagno Vignoni's thermal spa.
Bellissimo! ▶	Tuscan charmer with tip-top views.

Relais La Suvera
53030 Pievescola
Siena
T +39 0577 960 300
F +39 0577 960 220
E info@lasuvera.it
W lasuvera.it
Marchese Giuseppe Ricci
19 rooms, 13 suites
Rates €385-1,200
Dinner from €85

Closed 3 Nov – 13 April

Extras

Courtesy of
Room for Romance:
Wine and a basket of
fresh fruit in your room
on arrival.

Airport Florence (64 km)

Arrival From Florence: take A1,
then S2 for Siena. Exit at
Colle di Val d'Elsa and
follow Gracciano signs.
When there, go left for
Grasseto on SP541; after
15 km left for Pievescola.

Relais La Suvera

This medieval papal villa with fabulous views over the Chianti hills has been turned into a head-turning Tuscan hotel. Once the lavish home of Pope Julius II, Relais La Suvera has been owned by a line of counts and aristocrats over the centuries. Now home to Marquis Giuseppe Ricci and his wife Princess Eleonora Massimo, it's stuffed with art treasures and things of beauty. A signature three-storey Renaissance loggia, giant birdcage (but no caged birds), feast of classical statuary, vaulted and frescoed ceilings, private chapel and wealth of family antiques put it in a league of its own. Bedrooms are pure fantasy trips, with fabulously flamboyant beds, bronzes and paintings. Think four-posters swirled in silk tied to gilded pillars; soaring, ceiling height oil paintings; lamps mounted on classical columns; boudoirs framed in ruched gold-trimmed drapes; pyramids of plump pillows waiting to be dived into. Outside there's a beautiful pool shielded by cypress trees, a courtyard set with tables perfect for aperitifs, and a wellness centre where (if all this hasn't put you on a high) you can be pampered to bits.

Love time For sheer extravagance, disappear behind the doors of the Maria Gabriella di Savoia suite, with its Baroque mirrors and vast canopied bed.

Love bites Dine informally beneath the linden trees or go posh in the Oliviera restaurant.

Love it up You're an easy drive from historic Siena, Volterra and San Gimignano.

Bellissimo! ▶ Ravishing Renaissance villa shot through with romance.

Adler Thermae Spa & Wellness Resort
53027 Bagno Vignoni
San Quirico d'Orcia, Siena
T +39 0577 889 000
F +39 0577 889 999
E info@adler-thermae.com
W adler-thermae.com
Roland Margesin
90 rooms
Rates €340-386
Dinner: included in room price

Closed mid Jan – mid Feb

Extras Courtesy of
Room for Romance:
A bottle of prosecco
and strawberries in
your room.

Airport Florence (150 km)
Rome (200 km)
Pisa (250 km)

Arrival From Siena: take the S2
in direction of Rome until
you reach San Quirico
d'Orcia. Then follow signs
to Bagno Vignoni.

Adler Thermae

Get high just by breathing the air. The village of Bagno Vignoni sits between soft, green Tuscan hills scarcely changed since the Romans discovered the healing properties of its natural thermal waters. Wrapped in vapours rising from the pools that surround it, this fabulous spa hotel sprawls gently, a softly coloured, low-lying building in the style of a rural villa. Fresh, spacious, uncluttered bedrooms have a simple elegance with honey-coloured woods, creamy walls, shots of warm colours in the fabrics and dozens of fat white candles to soften the mood at nightfall. Be as indulgent or energetic as you like. Drift from thermal pool to herbal steam room to olive tree wood sauna, wallow in the Etruscan clay bath or disappear underground into the salt grotto. Take your pick of dozens of spa treatments – maybe an Ayurveda wrap, hot stone massage or salt scrub, or recline like Cleopatra with a milk and honey wrap on a waterbed. If the air has energised you, try a spot of outdoor yoga, Zen stretching or Pilates. What with the heady air and dreamy scenery, you'll feel pretty good about yourselves – and each other.

Love time	Soak in the deep tub in your marble bathroom, then open some vino on your private terrace with nothing but Tuscany to disturb the view.
Love bites	Dine under the stars in summer, and don't miss sensational afternoon teas.
Love it up	Try an Argillae clay bath for two, or pedal off on mountain bikes.
Bellissimo!	Superlative Tuscan spa that hits all the senses.

Hotel Monteriggioni
Via 1 Maggio 25
53035 Monteriggioni
T +39 577 305 009
F +39 577 305 011
E info@hotelmonteriggioni.net
W hotelmonteriggioni.net
Michela Cagnazzo
12 rooms
Rates €230

Closed 7 Jan – 28 Feb

Extras Courtesy of
Room for Romance:
A bottle of wine from
Fattoria Castello di
Monteriggioni.

Airport Florence (65 km)
Pisa (150 km)

Arrival From Florence: take
the S2 south, exit for
Monteriggioni, drive along
the SS2 for 1 km towards
Siena, then turn left.
Private parking.

Monteriggioni

This storybook castle-hamlet, whose original medieval walls are crowned by 14 towers, sits squarely on a hilltop above rolling countryside. It's quite a sight, and there's an array of Tuscan treasures on the doorstep – you're just a short drive from Siena, Florence, San Gimignano and the vineyards of Chianti. Encircled by remarkable 800-year-old stone ramparts (built in the 1200s to repel invading Florentines), Hotel Monteriggioni has been beautifully created from the castle's former stables. A doorway opens into a tall and spacious lobby with rooms leading off through broad stone archways. Beamed ceilings and smooth white walls characterise the 12 bedrooms, designed for comfort with elegant fabrics, wrought-iron bedsteads, handsome antiques and roomy bathrooms. Each one is different, and all are immaculate. Laze among the olive trees or cool off in the pool in the prettily landscaped gardens – the perfect place to read a book or gen up on Tuscan history. You'll get a great cosseting from staff at this peaceful little enclave with its off-the-beaten-track vibe.

Love time	Comfortable quarters await: time to pull down the drawbridge?
Love bites	Delicious breakfasts are served al fresco during summer. There's an excellent Tuscan restaurant just outside the hotel door.
Love it up	Hit the superstrada ten minutes away and Tuscany is ripe for exploration.

Bellissimo!	Picture-worthy castle-hamlet on Chianti's doorstep.

Villa Agnese
Viale Agostino Marti 177
55100 Lucca
T +39 0583 467 109
F +39 0583 464 048
E info@villagnese.it
W villagnese.it
Antonella Raspini
9 rooms
Rates €150-210

Open all year round

Extras   Courtesy of
Room for Romance:
A basket of fruit in your
room and a discount on
the standard room rate.

Airport   Pisa (20 km)

Arrival   From Pisa Airport: take
the A11 and A12 to
Lucca. The hotel is just off
the ring road circling the
old city, close to Porta
Santa Maria.

Villa Agnese

This classic Liberty style peach-coloured villa, with its handsome dark shutters, may liberate your senses. The flowing lines and emphasis on nature echo Italy's take on the early 20th century Art Nouveau movement, known as the Liberty years. Beautifully and meticulously restored, this discreet little hotel is just a meander away from Lucca's ancient city walls. Shiny parquet and marble floors are blended with soft pastels and neutrals in the welcoming hallway and intimate little bar. Furnishings are elegant and all eight bedrooms, with their pretty tiled bathrooms, are characterised by soothing colours and attention to detail. Two look over the road while the others (our favourites) overlook the luxuriant, flower-filled gardens where butterflies flit drowsily. Spoil yourself with drinks on the sun-dappled terrace and be mesmerised by Lucca's walls as the light constantly changes their colour. And, at sunset, a stroll around the walls is a brilliant experience. Puccini, creator of those operatic giants Tosca and Madama Butterfly, was born not far from here. We're tempted to think that a touch of that artistry lingers on.

Love time Cool green Menta is the largest room. Others have sunny Tuscan charm.
Love bites Enjoy buffet-style breakfasts in the charming dining room or pretty garden.
Love it up Take bicycles for two, provided by the Villa, and uncover the delights
concealed within the walls of richly medieval Lucca.

Bellissimo! ▶ Peachy villa in classic park setting.

UMBRIA

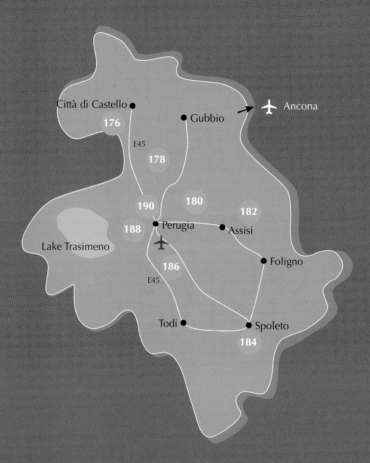

Città di Castello •
176
E45
178
• Gubbio
✈ Ancona
180
190
182
188
• Perugia
✈
• Assisi
Lake Trasimeno
186
• Foligno
E45
Todi •
• Spoleto
184

LOVE IT This is quintessential Italy: a wealth of fabulous medieval hilltop towns, mist-cloaked hills, deep valleys and artistic treasures. Charm-laden Umbria is also dubbed Tuscany without the tourists. **When to go** Try autumn and winter, when it's mountain-crisp outside and fireside-warm within. **Don't miss** Wandering through the history-steeped hilltop towns of Assisi, Gubbio, Spoleto and Todi – just some of the medieval gems rich in art and architecture. Join pilgrims visiting Assisi's shrine of St Francis, sip a cappuccino in Todi's Piazza del Popolo – possibly Italy's most perfect piazza – wander Gubbio's 13th century streets, or walk in untamed woodlands where deer and wild boar roam. Chocoholics should head for Perugia, home of the Perugina Baci – Italy's famous sweet-tooth treat. **Dine on** Game is plentiful, and be sure to try porchetta – stuffed roast suckling pig. Other signature dishes include tartufi neri – black truffles stuffed into ravioli and mixed in risotto. **Drink up** Great local wines include Orvieto, Montefalco Rosso, Colli Perugini and Torgiano.

QUINTESSENTIAL HILLTOP TOWNS

Pages 176-191

Palazzo Terranova
Località Ronti Morra
06010 Perugia
T +39 075 857 0083
F +39 075 857 0014
E bookings@palazzoterranova.com
W palazzoterranova.com
Sarah and Johnny Townsend
12 rooms
Rates €295-795
Dinner from €70

Open all year round

Extras Courtesy of Room for Romance: Upgrade on arrival if available.

Airport Perugia (50 km)
Florence (108 km)
Forli (140 km)

Arrival From Citta di Castello: follow signs to Trestina. At Ronti, right after cemetery, left at junction, then right at large tree onto unmade road; 2 km to hotel.

Palazzo Terranova

Climbing the steep dirt track to Palazzo Terranova on a wet and wild autumn night felt like driving towards the edge of the world. It was the next morning when we clambered out of our vast wrought-iron bed and flung open the shutters to crisp October sunshine, gazing at a vista of wooded hills skirted in swirls of white cloud below us. It was both magical and mesmerising. Crowning an Umbrian hilltop with ravishing views, Palazzo Terranova is one of those utterly rare and special finds. Owner Sarah Townsend has brought this once dilapidated manor house back to life with passion and vision, filling it with art and antiques, fine paintings and things of beauty. It's now a dream for all seasons – a place dedicated to the good things in life. Sprawling bedrooms have huge armoires, deep travertine stone bathtubs and hand-painted panelling. Outside you can wander through landscaped grounds, sip champagne on the terrace, or float in the stunning infinity pool. There's a sociable house-party atmosphere, with guests gathering for drinks in the bar, dogs snoozing by the fire, and cooking that's as knockout as the surrounds.

Love time   Sneak off to bed early: super-sized beds are dressed in softest cottons.
Love bites   Head chef Honor cooks fabulous seasonal Italian dishes with style and flair: hand-made pappardelle, locally caught wild boar, succulent steaks.
Love it up   Wander hilltop paths, or explore historic Perugia, Assisi and Gubbio.

Bellissimo!   Sumptuous *palazzo paradiso* in the heart of Renaissance Italy.

Locanda del Gallo
Località Santa Cristina
06024 Gubbio
T +39 075 922 9912
F +39 075 922 9912
E info@locandadelgallo.it
W locandadelgallo.it
Paola Moro and Erich Breuer
10 rooms
Rates €112-132
Dinner from €60

Open all year round

Airport   Perugia (25 km)
Florence (150 km)
Rome Fiumicino (180 km)

Arrival   From Florence: take the
A1 south. Exit at Val di
Chiana, follow signs to
Perugia, then Cesena.
Exit at Ponte Pattoli, Casa
del Diavolo, then Santa
Cristina. From Rome: take
A1 north, exit at Orte,
follow signs to Perugia,
then Cesena, then as
above.

Locanda del Gallo

Winding our way through the Umbrian hills, we spied Locanda del Gallo from afar, nuzzled among trees and gazing out at a show-stopping vista of woods and valleys. Miles from the madding crowd, it's just the place to recharge and refresh. Owner Paola Moro has teamed the original 17th century farmhouse's rustic rafters and stone walls with Balinese teak furniture, carved wooden masks, art and oriental artefacts to beguiling effect. That's not all that makes Locanda del Gallo a cracking roost. Cockerels are everywhere – over 400 of them. Made from glass, wood and brightly painted ceramic, they perch on shelves, swing from mobiles and crow from picture frames. What with warm provençal walls, comfy four-poster beds and deep baths, the result is guaranteed to make you feel sunny side up. Utterly peaceful gardens dotted with sunloungers, a stunning shady verandah, astonishingly beautiful pool terrace, and delicious organic fare (everything from the bread to the yoghurt is made here) make this an ideal spot to revitalise jaded souls. There's even a little chapel in the grounds to say thanksgiving.

Love time   Bedrooms – all different – effortlessly mix rustic Italian with oriental ethnic.
Love bites   Chef Jimmy is a whizz at rustling up anything from tagliatelle al pesto to a fiery Indonesian stir-fry, conjuring up a different fixed menu nightly.
Love it up   Get walking – there are trails galore nearby – swim, or book a massage.

Bellissimo! Little Umbrian cracker with plenty to crow about.

Relais alla Corte del Sole
Località I Giorgi
06061 Petrignano del Lago
T +39 075 968 9008
F +39 075 968 9070
E info@cortedelsole.com
W cortedelsole.com
Ilaria Spiganti
17 rooms
Rates €160-210
Dinner from €80

Closed 10-31 January

Extras   Courtesy of
Room for Romance:
A welcome drink:
sparkling wine or an
aperitif.

Airport   Rome Fiumicino (170 km)
Florence (120 km)

Arrival   From Florence: take A1
south, exit at Val di Chiana,
then Perugia, followed by
Cortona, Montepulciano.
Then turn left to the
village of Petrignano.

Relais alla Corte del Sole

Slip through wrought-iron gates into the rich world of the Renaissance. This 16th century rosy cluster of buildings, arched windows and pantiled roofs surrounded by a centuries old olive grove, offers a timeless slice of Tuscany. Once you've crossed the threshold, you have no choice but to relax. Original features have been preserved – beamed ceilings, wooden doors, terracotta tiled floors – but mixed with antiques, paintings and tapestries to create a rustic elegance. No two bedrooms are the same – perhaps a chaise longue, a gilded mirror or a lacy covered table for breakfast à deux – yet all shamelessly cosset with rich fabrics, polished antiques, bowls of fruit and flowers. In the evening, lights dance around the walls from dozens of candles and flickering wall sconces. And did we mention the bathrooms? Nothing less than marbled and frescoed flights of fancy. Tuscany's art treasure towns are easily reached but you may find it hard to leave the perfumed garden with rose bowers, mossy sculptures and urns of tumbling flowers. At night, glowing with soft lights, it's the perfect setting for a lovers' tryst over chilled prosecco.

Love time   A canopied bed, scrolled bedhead, four-poster and soft muslin… take your pick. To turn up the heat, book a suite with a working fire.

Love bites   Tuscan cuisine is served in the glow of oil paintings and silky peach walls.

Love it up   Take a personally tailored wine-tasting tour to sample fine local vintages.

Bellissimo!   Tuscan tranquillity in an enchanted garden.

Le Silve di Armenzano
Località Armenzano
06081 Assisi
T +39 075 801 9000
F +39 075 801 9005
E info@lesilve.it
W lesilve.it
15 rooms
Marco Sirignani
Rates €166-182
Dinner from €80

Closed 15 November – mid March

Extras Courtesy of Room for Romance: A complimentary chilled bottle of champagne in your room.

Airport Ancona (90 km)
Rome Fiumicino (150 km)

Arrival From Assisi: follow signs for Gualdo-Taldino and watch for right hand fork signed Armenzano. Hotel is 2 km past the village, through electronic gates.

Le Silve

Finding Le Silve after climbing through miles of twisting country lanes is like stumbling on Shangri-La in the middle of nowhere. High in the startlingly beautiful Subasio national park and buried amid folds of rugged hills, it's as serene a spot as you could hope to find. The cluster of centuries-old stone farmhouses sits on a grassy promontory with views to die for. This is the heart of rural Umbria: wild deer roam in the woods, horses graze in grassy paddocks, mouflon sheep nibble on rocky slopes and walking trails melt away into the woods. Despite the hotel's blissfully remote location, there's no compromising on creature comforts within. A fire crackles in the huge fireplace of the reception on cool nights, while bedrooms have plenty of rustic charm. Dining is a high point at Le Silve, and this is the place to sample terrific home-cured meats and other dishes made from produce grown on the estate. Make time for an aperitif on the stunning terrace before dining within warm candlelit surrounds or beneath a giant canopy on summer nights.

Love time   Whitewashed walls, old terracotta tiled floors and beamed ceilings create pleasingly country quarters for bedding down.

Love bites   Our dinner of swordfish and pomegranate salad, cappellaci with rabbit sauce and home-reared crispy pork was first-rate.

Love it up   There's a wonderfully secluded pool, tennis courts and walking trails.

Bellissimo!   Just the place to watch the sun set over the Umbrian hills.

Villa Milani
Località Colle Attivoli 4
06049 Spoleto
T +39 0743 225 056
F +39 0743 49824
E info@villamilani.com
W villamilani.com
Luigi and Giovanna Capobianchi
11 rooms
Rates €190-380
Dinner from €110

Closed early January – early February

Extras

Airport

Arrival

Courtesy of
Room for Romance:
A 10% discount on
published room rates.

Rome Fiumicino (160 km)

From Rome: leave the A1
for Firenze at Orte, then
follow signs to Terni-
Spoleto. In Spoleto take
first exit for town, follow
signs to Torricella and
look out for signs leading
uphill to the villa (1.5 km).

Villa Milani

We arrived at Villa Milani – a peach-perfect Italianate villa crowning a hilltop above historic Spoleto – soon after the departure of an awesome US rock musician, who had swept in from New York with his wife just for three nights to mark their wedding anniversary. That's an indication of how special Villa Milani is. This family-owned 19th century hillside hideaway has been lavished with TLC and now glows with expensive Renaissance charm. Exuberant, swirling gilded columns, bronze cherubs, antique clocks, wonderfully embellished ceilings and a huge stone fireplace make the lounge feel like part of a private palace. Step outside and you are in beautiful parkland dotted with fountains and classical statues, with the rooftops and spires of medieval Spoleto – one of Umbria's gems – flung at your feet and views beyond of softly wooded hills. Named after the constellations, rooms are beautifully decorated with original shutters, antique carved bedheads and handsome, polished wood furniture. With unsurpassed views over Spoleto's twinkling lights, the gardens beg for sunset strolls and stolen kisses.

Love time	Take the utterly private Tower suite: just you, the bed and the birdsong.
Love bites	Enjoy breakfast on the terrace, in your room or indoors in cooler months.
Love it up	Float in the curvaceous infinity pool, walk Spoleto's ancient city walls or take one of the hotel's classic sports cars for a spin.

Bellissimo!   A taste of the good life in classic hilltop setting.

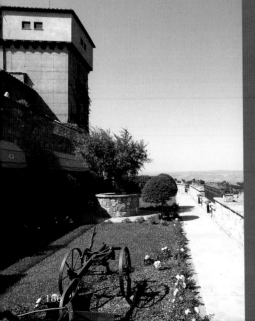

Relais Il Canalicchio
Via della Piazza 4
06050 Canalicchio
T +39 075 870 7325
F +39 075 870 7296
E relais@relaisilcanalicchio.it
W relaisilcanalicchio.it
Federico Pittaluga
49 rooms
Rates €195-256
Dinner from €90

Closed late November – late December

Extras

Courtesy of
Room for Romance:
A glass of prosecco on
arrival.

Airport

Rome Fiumicino (170 km)

Arrival

From Rome: take the A1
highway north towards
Terni, exiting at Orte onto
the E45 Perugia dual
carriageway. Take the
Ripabianca-Foligno exit
and follow signs for a
further 8 km.

Relais Il Canalicchio

Leave the motorway behind and climb up and away into the hills – high enough and far enough to make you wonder if you've taken a wrong turn. Finally you're there – a medieval hamlet-turned-hotel clustered on a hilltop with lyrical views over the Umbrian countryside. The old castello, with its distinctive square tower and stone archways, dominates the scene. Inside you'll find beamed ceilings, terracotta tiled floors, giant fireplaces and remnants of the castle's agricultural past. Rooms are named after British nobility, so don't be surprised to find yourself bedding down with the Countess of Oxford or the Duke of Buckingham. There's a touch of English country house about everything, with pretty floral wallcoverings and bedspreads, and geranium-fringed balconies. We loved the roomy new country suites, with their pastel shades, stencilled walls and rustic furniture, landscaped around a pool away from the main building. An open brazier warms Il Pavone restaurant, where it's all fine napery, candlelight and good regional cooking given a contemporary twist. Outside there's hardly a passing car to disturb the peace.

Love time	Soak in the suds of your jacuzzi bath in one of the airy country suites.
Love bites	Tasty house specialities include wild boar sausages, home-cured salami and risotto with truffles. Try a slug of the house grappa as a chaser.
Love it up	There's a gym, billiard room, tennis, walking trails and riding for starters.
Bellissimo!	Hilltop castello turned hotel with poetic views.

Locanda Solomeo Country House
Piazza Carlo Alberto Dalla Chiesa 1
06073 Solomeo, Perugia
T +39 075 529 3119
F +39 075 529 4090
E solomeo@tin.it
W solomeo.it
Pier Luigi and Donatella Cavicchi
12 rooms
Rates €99-125
Dinner from €60

Closed 8 Jan – 28 Feb and 24-26 Dec

Extras

Airport

Arrival

Courtesy of
Room for Romance:
A bottle of sparkling wine
in your room, fresh fruit
and a late checkout.

Perugia (25 km)
Rome Fiumicino (170 km)
Florence (150 km)

From Florence: take A1
south towards Perugia, go
right at Corciano exit.
Follow signs to Solomeo;
hotel is in main square.

Locanda Solomeo

The sleepy hilltop village of Solomeo is Umbria's cashmere capital. And just across the street from where some of Italy's swankiest woollies are woven is Locanda Solomeo, a buttercup-yellow late 19th century villa shielded by trees. Owners Donatella and Pier Luigi Cavicchi have done a wonderful job of restoring the turn-of-the-century house with its sweeping views since acquiring it 15 years ago, and the place has oodles of charm. You almost expect a Baroque quartet to be strumming away in the cosy Mazzerioli tea room with its fetchingly pretty floor-to-ceiling frescoes and swags. Bedrooms are rustic-pretty, with painted shutters and wood panelling, stencilled wall motifs, pleasing fabrics and well tricked-out bathrooms with every comfort. Downstairs there's a sunnily painted restaurant dotted with fresh flowers, serving tasty regional cooking with hand-made pasta and farm-fresh organic veggies. Pier Luigi stocks an impressive selection of Umbrian wines. Dine on the terrace in warm weather, then sleep off your indulgences by the secluded pool and soak up the tranquillity.

Love time   Pretty drapes and original antiques make for quaint and cosy quarters.
Love bites   Nibble on freshly-baked cakes, or dine amid the olive groves on the terrace.
Love it up   Trawl for cashmeres or head to historic Perugia, a 20 minute drive away.
Staff can organise trips to local wine cellars and olive oil mills.

Bellissimo!   Blissful little find in a rural timewarp.

Castello dell'Oscano
Strada della Forcella 37
06010 Cenerente, Perugia
T +39 075 584 371
F +39 075 690 666
E info@oscano.com
W oscano.com
Michele Ravano & Maurizio Bussolati
11 rooms
Rates €150-320
Dinner from €70

Open all year round

Extras Courtesy of
Room for Romance:
A room upgrade subject
to availability.

Airport   Florence (120 km)
Rome Fiumicino (170 km)

Arrival   From Florence: take the
A1 south, follow
directions to Perugia, then
turn left and follow
directions to Cerenente
and blue signs to the
castle.

Castello dell'Oscano

Stroll around the battlements, dine in the glow of rich wood panelling, sink into the deepest of sofas. This is no-holds barred, traditional Italian country house living. The neo-Gothic 18th century castle, built on 14th century foundations, will fulfil your aristocratic fantasies – towers, parapets, hidden courtyards, vaulted ceilings, shuttered windows, grand staircases and acres of polished wood abound. Together with the next door 19th century villa, it overlooks rolling Umbrian countryside as well as its own wooded parkland. A fleet of ground floor rooms – including a library, several sitting rooms and a lofty hallway – are scattered with antiques, marble fireplaces, mirrors and rich rugs on polished floors. It's chintzy, snug (in a grand sort of way), unstuffy and gorgeously indolent. You could drift from breakfast through to dinner with the help of a good book, a glass of wine and not notice the time. Upstairs, bedrooms are vast, full of elegant antiques, big windows, old-fashioned grandeur and carved fireplaces. In Villa Ada rooms have a lighter, classical touch. With fruit, flowers, rich fabrics, soft lights and uninterrupted views, there's just enough to feel indulged without it going over the top.

Love time   Fling open the shutters and let the moonlight in: your privacy is assured.
Love bites   This is Italian dining as it should be – in a setting of classical elegance.
Love it up   Test your tastebuds with an olive oil tasting in the estate's ancient oil press.

Bellissimo!   Live like a laid-back aristocrat.

ROME & LAZIO

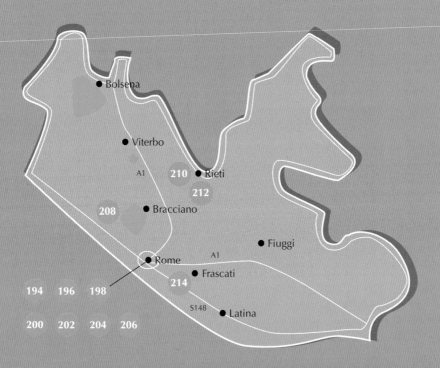

- Bolsena
- Viterbo
- A1
- 210 Rieti
- 212
- 208
- Bracciano
- Fiuggi
- Rome
- A1
- 214 Frascati
- 194 196 198
- S148
- Latina
- 200 202 204 206

LOVE IT Say *Buongiorno* to Michelangelo, Leonardo and Raphael: Rome is a banquet of classical art and sculpture stuffed with ancient history. Forget the chaotic traffic – toss coins in the Trevi fountain and know you'll return.
When to go May, June and September are the best months. August can be a scorcher – but as the city empties out there are terrific hotel deals to be had. **Don't miss** All roads lead to Rome… and you can't leave town without seeing blockbuster sights like the Colosseum, Sistine Chapel, Spanish Steps, the Trevi fountain (wonderfully photo-genic), or the Catacombs (wonderfully creepy). Via Veneto is the last word in shopping, so load up your plastic. Further afield? See Villa D'Este in Tivoli, the wine town of Frascati, and dip your toes in Lake Bracciano. **Dine on** Thin-crust pizza Romana or local pasta dishes: bucatini all'amatriciana comes with spicy tomato sauce and bacon. Romans love offal, so be brave and try trippa (tripe) and cervello (brains), or osso buco (shin of veal). **Drink up** Have a chilled caffè freddo in a café on Piazza Navona and watch Rome at play.

POPES, PALAZZI AND A CAPITAL RETREAT

Pages 194-215

Casa Howard
Via Capo Le Case 18 / Via Sistina 149
00187 Rome
T +39 0669 924 555
F +39 0667 94644
E info@casahoward.it
W casahoward.com
Jenifer Howard Forneris
5 rooms at each address
Rates €160–230, breakfast €12

Airport Rome Fiumicino or
Ciampino (both 25 km)

Arrival Via Sistina and Via Capo
Le Case are both a
stone's throw from the
Spanish Steps in the old
centro storico. Nearest
metro station: Piazza di
Spagna.

Open all year round

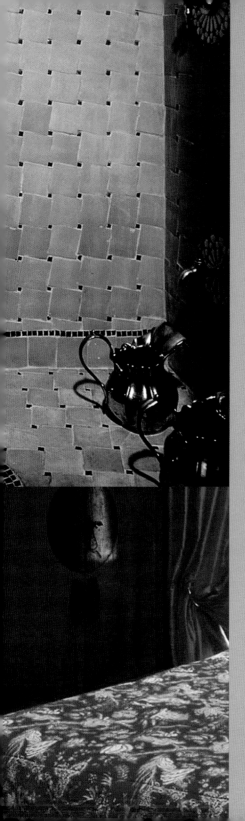

Casa Howard

We're rather taken with Casa Howard's split personality. One half comprises five rooms on the Capo le Case, while the other occupies the second floor of an old palazzo on Via Sistina. You'll find the pair between the Spanish Steps and the Trevi Fountain – so expect liveliness plus all the feel of private homes. These flamboyant B&Bs are more like the pied-à-terre of some top interior designer. Owners Count Leonardi and wife Jenifer Howard Forneris have set out to create intimate establishments with five-star style. Their leisure-plus-pleasure philosophy certainly works. Two housekeepers, or 'house genies', attend and cosset. Nice touches abound: fresh flowers, immaculate linens, Florentine soaps, kimonos, an honesty bar and private keys. Both places even enjoy hammams. But it's the rooms themselves that exemplify the owners' philosophy: think country-house meets ethnic meets modern-retro. There's the zany Zebra room, all black and white on red; the White room's extravaganza in toile de Jouy; the swathing silks of the Chinese room. Throw in bespoke furniture, antiques and pictures, and the whole effect is seductive and – dare we say it – stylishly schizophrenic. There's even a sister property in Florence.

Love time   In Via Sistina the Flower room's delightful floral riot has a hammam.
Love bites   It's breakfast in bed here: freshly baked *cornetti* and home-made jams.
Love it up   Jennifer's list of must-sees has great off-the-beaten-track recommendations.

Bellissimo! ☛   Wham-bam designer glam.

Hotel Hassler
Piazza Trinità dei Monti 6
00187 Rome
T +39 0669 9340
F +39 0667 89991
W hotelhasslerroma.com
E booking@hotelhassler.com
Roberto E Wirth
98 rooms and suites
Rates €616-935
Dinner from €280

Airport   Rome Ciampino (15 km)
              Rome Fiumicino (32 km)

Arrival   The hotel is at the top of
              the Spanish Steps on
              Piazza Trinità dei Monti,
              next to the church.
              Nearest metro station:
              Piazza di Spagna.

Open all year round

Hotel Hassler

Plush, elegant and impeccably mannered, the Hassler is indisputably one of Rome's grande dames. With staff constantly at your beck and call and a fleet of limos at the door it's no wonder royalty, presidents and stars flock here. With its unassailable position atop the Piazza di Spagna, lording it over the city's rooftops and the Villa Medici garden, you'll adore buying into the Hassler lifestyle, however briefly. The classically decorated interior, newly refurbished, gets full marks. Dramatic Venetian lamps and Murano chandeliers cast soft light over marble pillars and ornate plasterwork. Salons with intricate tapestries, frescoes and mosaics counterpoint fine upholstered furniture and works of art. Suites maintain the richness, mixed with contemporary accents. Rome's skyline is almost on your plate at the famed Rooftop restaurant, one of the city's premier culinary landmarks, while the concierge desk has the keys to anything and everything. The Hassler has not surprisingly been showered in awards over the years, and it's easy to see why.

Love time   Money to burn? The star-worthy Trinità dei Monti suite boasts floor-to ceiling windows and five wrap-around balconies.

Love bites   Chef Francesco Apreda's menus showcase Italian classics with added zest.

Love it up   Wallow in the hotel's wellness centre before storming Gucci, Valentino, Armani et al… quite aside from Rome's cultural glories.

Bellissimo! 💗   Imperial luxury fit for a Roman emperor.

Il Palazzetto
Vicolo del Bottino 8
00187 Rome
T +39 0669 934 301
F +39 0669 941 607
E respalaz@hotelhassler.it
W wineacademyroma.com
Roberto E Wirth
4 rooms
Rates €215-345
Dinner from €120

Airport   Rome Ciampino (15 km)
Rome Fiumicino (32 km)

Arrival   The hotel is in Vicolo del
Bottino, a small street
leading off Piazza di
Spagna. Nearest metro
station: Spagna.

Open all year round

Il Palazzetto

If you love your wine, you'll adore Il Palazzetto – aka The International Wine Academy of Roma. This 16th century palazzo dramatically overlooks the Spanish Steps: any closer and you'd be standing on them. Stylishly converted into a private club by owners Hotel Hassler next door (guests can use the latter's amenities) it has just four enticing suites. A centrepiece spiral staircase leads to the beautifully appointed salon, restaurant and wine bar, while an ivy-clad garden and brilliant roof terrace add extra appeal. Come here simply to enjoy Rome or come to hone your knowledge of all things wine: join a course led by resident wine experts, listen to guest speakers, take a guided tasting, sign up for master classes in wine appreciation or join a trip to a leading wine estate. Whether or not you come to quaff some of the cellar's 400-odd labels, you'll love simply staying. Dripping with voluptuous fabrics and soft furnishings, suites define classic-meets-contemporary chic. There's fabulous terrace dining – matched flawlessly by wines, of course – and should you tire of drinking, the pinnacles of fashion and Roman history await outside.

Love time   Bury yourselves in indulgent velvet-covered beds piled with silken cushions.
Love bites   Masterchef Antonio Martucci draws flavours from impeccably sourced ingredients for Italian dishes with a twist.
Love it up   The list of options is a corker: tastings, tuition, vineyards or simply imbibing.

Bellissimo! ▶   Wine lovers' haven with full-bodied finish.

Hotel Locarno
Via della Penna 22
00186 Rome
T +39 0636 10841
F +39 0632 15249
E info@hotellocarno.com
W hotellocarno.com
Caterina Valente
66 rooms
Rates €220-310

Open all year round

Extras

Courtesy of
Room for Romance:
A complimentary chilled
bottle of champagne in
your room (if deluxe).

Airport

Rome Ciampino (15 km)

Arrival

The hotel is in the centre
of Rome, close to Piazza
del Popolo. Nearest metro
station: Flaminio.

Hotel Locarno

This Art Deco style temple near the Piazza del Popolo is something of a mecca for writers, actors and the movie set. It was the set for Bernard Weber's film Hotel Locarno back in the '70s, and still retains much of its original 1920s flavour. The hotel's understated shabby-chic style, wealth of period detailing and air of faded elegance have made it one of the neighbourhood's hot addresses. Mother and daughter owners Maria Teresa and Caterina have filled the hotel with antiques bought from fairs and auctions around Italy: you'll find an original birdcage lift, Tiffany lamps, gleaming original mosaic and parquet floors. They also acquired the next door apartment building a few years ago, and rooms in this wing are not only a tad quieter but stylish indeed. Four deluxe rooms with lofty ceilings have fantasy wallpapers, ornate ceilings, silken cushions and vast stately bathrooms. Those in the main building are more homespun, with soft colours and nicely coordinated fabrics. There's a panoramic roof garden to take in the views, and if Rome's traffic doesn't phase you, the hotel's bikes are there for a spin around the neighbourhood.

Love time   You're staying in a vintage movie set: just play the stars or rewrite the plot.
Love bites   Enjoy a chilled *aperitivo* – in the sunny courtyard garden or up on the roof.
Love it up   You're just a few minutes from the Spanish Steps and the designer shopping emporia of Via Condotti.

Bellissimo! ▶   Art Deco charmer with star appeal.

Hotel de Russie
Via del Babuino 9
00187 Rome
T +39 0632 8881
F +39 0632 888 888
E reservations@hotelderussie.it
W hotelderussie.it
Elena Bruno
90 rooms, 33 suites
Rates €615-2,700
Dinner from €120

Airport Rome Ciampino (15 km)
Rome Fiumicino (32 km)

Arrival The hotel is located in the city centre, between the Spanish Steps and Piazza del Popolo. Nearest metro station: Flaminio.

Open all year round

Hotel de Russie

When famed hotelier Sir Rocco Forte nabbed this derelict building in the city's heart five years ago it could have become another of those corporately smart but so-what places. Now the epitome of understated glamour, it oozes drop-dead chic. While the defining look is contemporary, there are classic twists too. A striking lobby with an unpolished marble floor greets guests; furniture is symbolic of the best Italian design, walls are accented with signed Mapplethorpe photographs. Reception leads to a magnificent secret garden whose palms, orange trees and climbing roses stretch towards the Pincino hillside. The see-and-be-seen Le Jardin restaurant, in a palette of reds hinting at Belle Epoque, is a hot watering hole; ditto the Stravinskij Bar, under the eye of an enormous abstract. Guests who crave further indulgence can head for the spa or call on concierge services to make things happen (as they do for Sir Elton, Naomi, Julia Roberts and George Clooney). Staff look as if they love working here and service, as you would expect, is spot-on. No doubt about it – the de Russie is de business.

Love time   The terraced, top-floor Picasso suite is all full-on luxury and technics.
Love bites   Le Jardin restaurant is palpably fashionable, with quintessential Italian cuisine.
Love it up   Imperial Rome? Shop-to-drop Nirvana? Holy Roman Empire? All roads lead to whichever Rome you want (the concierge sees to it!).

Bellissimo! ▶   Latin buzz, Forte elegance, Italian chic.

Hotel Santa Maria
Vicolo del Piede 2
00153 Rome
T +39 0658 94626
F +39 0658 94815
E info@hotelsantamaria.info
W hotelsantamaria.info
Paolo Vetere
18 rooms
Rates €220

Open all year round

Extras

Courtesy of
Room for Romance:
A bottle of sparkling wine
and a 10% discount on
room rates.

Airport

Rome Fiumicino (32 km)
Rome Ciampino (15 km)

Arrival

The hotel is a few steps
from Piazza Trastevere
and easy to reach by bus.
Car drivers should call for
directions. Parking close
by, €15 per day.

204

Santa Maria

Rome's Trastevere district still has a richly medieval feel: tall houses packed hugger-mugger within a labyrinth of uneven cobbled streets. The Santa Maria – a former convent – hides itself in one such. We pressed the bell on an anonymous-looking door which snapped open to spill us unexpectedly into a pretty pebbled square filled with light. The hotel has been converted from what was originally a 16th century convent and still maintains the sense of being cloistered away. At the heart is the eponymous courtyard, sprinkled with orange trees and an abundance of flowers. Parasoled tables provide shade but there are pockets where you can sun-soak too. An artisan's workshop is now the dining room, and we flitted happily in and out with bottles from their well-stocked cellar. Come evening, the streets around here fill with the tables of good-value osterias; for dessert we called into one of the icecream parlours for our nightly shot of gelato. Here's a place in an area with some buzz that feels utterly tranquil.

Love time   Bedrooms and spacious mansard-roofed duplexes open onto the courtyard.

Love bites   A refectory table groans with breakfast goodies, while the complimentary afternoon buffet is a nice touch.

Love it up   Get lost in the area's higgledy-piggledy streets, before crossing the river to Isola Tiberina and the old Jewish quarter.

Bellissimo!   Fabulous little find you wouldn't know was there.

Hotel Villa San Pio
Via Santa Melania 19
00153 Rome
T +39 0657 0057
F +39 0657 41112
E info@aventinohotels.com
W aventinohotels.com
Roberta Piroli
78 rooms
Rates €140-220
Dinner from €70

Open all year round

Extras Courtesy of
Room for Romance:
A complimentary bottle of
prosecco in your room.

Airport Rome Fiumicino (30 km)

Arrival From Termini rail station:
take Via Cavour, then
San Gregorio and Viale
Aventino. Via Santa
Melania is on the right.
Nearest metro station:
Circo Massimo.

Villa San Pio

Escape the hubbub of central Rome at the San Pio, a converted villa surrounded by serene green gardens on Aventine Hill. The area is mainly residential but you can lay Rome at your lover's feet with some of the finest views in the city. This recently refurbished hotel is quietly elegant without trying too hard, its spacious lobby decorated with stained glass and fine objets d'arts. Rooms are generally large, prettily and soothingly decorated in creams and golds, with traditional furniture, embroidered bedcovers, painted doors and glamorous marble bathrooms with jacuzzi baths; some have private balconies or terraces. In season, the gardens are heady with the scent of roses while the trickle of the fountain is a world away from city traffic. Drink in the tranquillity over a generous breakfast al fresco or indoors on cool days in the conservatory dining room. The hotel is within easy distance of all the main sights, with a bus stop just outside and the metro a ten-minute walk away. Staff are helpful and hospitable, as is the hotel's friendly cat.

Love time   We loved Room 530, with its jacuzzi bath and wrap-around terrace.
Love bites   On a balmy summer's night the candlelit tables in the gardens are just the place for a midnight digestif.
Love it up   Swear eternal love in the Aventine Hill's rose garden, or the nearby Parco degli Arancia (orange grove). The sights of Rome are a short bus ride away.

Bellissimo! ➤   Calm neighbourhood oasis tailor-made for restful Roman holiday.

Hotel Villa Clementina
Via Traversa Quarto del Lago 12
00062 Bracciano
T/F +39 069 986 268
E villaclementina@tiscali.it
W hotelvillaclementina.it
Dimitri Bonetti
7 rooms
Rates €135-270
Dinner from €84

Open all year round

Extras
Courtesy of
Room for Romance:
A bottle of Casale Cento
Corvi wine (red or white)
in your room.

Airport
Rome Fiumicino (30 km)

Arrival
From Rome Fiumicino
Airport: take the A12
motorway towards
Civitavecchia and exit at
Cerveteri. Follow signs for
Bracciano; hotel is signed
from there.

Villa Clementina

Picture a small group of rustic but elegant Etruscan country houses spilling over three tiers of lush gardens, in the depths of the Lazio countryside. Then sketch in Villa Clementina's dreamy location beside shimmering Lake Bracciano, 30 km north of Rome. It's here that owner and artist Dimitri Bonetti conducts art courses in a lovely light-filled atelier and in the open air. Not that you need to be a budding Da Vinci to relish a stay at this delightful whitewashed country house just a half-hour from Rome. There are ravishing gardens splashed with bougainvillea and an enticing pool shielded by tall trees that simply invites a post-lunch siesta, not to mention a parasol-shaded terrace perfect for drinks or al fresco breakfasts. The country-kitchen restaurant, with its painted furniture, jugs of fresh flowers and large chimneypiece, is the setting for tasty regional cuisine using locally grown organic produce. Bedroom walls sport engaging murals, each with a different theme. Here's a *simpatico* little enclave where guests, whether arty or not, can recharge batteries in bucolic surroundings.

Love time   Wonderfully spacious rooms are distinctively themed with painted frescoes.
Love bites   The kitchen's more-ish specialities include linguine all'Amalfitana, risotto with porcini, and wood-fired pizzas. Guests dine al fresco when it's fine.
Love it up   Sail or windsurf on Lake Bracciano, or head off to the Eternal city.

Bellissimo! ❧   Little masterpiece by Lake Bracciano.

Borgo Paraelios
Valle Collicchia
02040 Poggio Catino, Rieti
T +39 0765 26267
F +39 0765 26268
info@borgoparaelios.it
borgoparaelios.it
Andrea Salabe
16 rooms, 2 junior suites
Rates €300
Dinner from €120

Closed November – February

Extras

Airport

Arrival

Courtesy of
Room for Romance:
A complimentary chilled
bottle of prosecco.

Rome Ciampino (70 km)
Rome Fiumicino (100 km)

From A1 highway: exit at
Ponzano/Soratti and after
tollgate go straight for 3 km
to Poggio Mirteto, then
right onto SS657 towards
Cantalupo-Terni and left
at T junction for Terni.

Borgo Paraelios

Leave behind the heat and the hassle of Rome, weave your way high into the cool of the Sabine Hills, and into the welcoming arms of this 19th century country villa wrapped in olive groves and cypress trees. You'll feel as good as a Roman patrician as you wander along its flower-filled avenue, through the columned entrance and into the elegant, sumptuous salons filled with deep sofas, rugs on ancient polished terracotta floors, huge open fireplaces, and walls hung with tapestries, Canalettos and Attardis. With piles of books, a billiard room and cosy library, it feels like a rather grand family home. Which, indeed, it is. Bedrooms are soft, warm spaces of peach, apricot, lemon and green. Brass beds, plump cushions, gleaming antiques and rich floral fabrics add to the country house feel while bowls of fresh flowers and beautiful cut glass add personal touches. The restaurant is all crisp white cloths, richly upholstered chairs and elegantly rustic cooking. Rome is less than an hour away but with an indoor and outdoor pool, golf course, spa and woodland walks, why leave?

Love time   Breakfast on your private garden patio is the only way to start the day.
Love bites   Dine beneath frescoes and a vaulted wooden ceiling – or, in summer, beneath the stars.
Love it up   Walk, book a spa treatment or spend a day doing Rome's capital sights.

Bellissimo!   The perfect Roman retreat.

Villa Sanguigni
Frazione Bagnolo
02012 Amatrice, Rieti
T/F +39 0746 821 075
E sanguigni1@libero.it
W primitaly.it/bb/villasanguigni
Domenico Sanguigni
5 rooms
Rates €90-100

Closed November and February

Extras

Courtesy of
Room for Romance:
Welcome champagne and
a 10% discount if staying
for five nights or more.

Airport

Pescara (100 km)
Rome (148 km)

Arrival

From Rome: take the S4
towards Ascoli Piceno
until the sign at 129 km
for Bagnolo. The Villa is on
the right hand side just as
you enter the village.

Villa Sanguigni

It takes your breath away up here. This great little B&B benefits from a terrific location within sight of the snow-dusted Laga Mountains. Lovingly tended – as are the gardens around it – it's the ancestral home of the Orlandi-Sanguigni family, sitting high on the edge of Bagnolo di Amatrice, an almost peasant-like hamlet 100 km north of Rome. The owners are warm and engaging and these very characteristics imbue their home. The interior delightfully mixes the rustic with the sophisticated – expect town and country antiques, pictures and rugs that set off wood floors and rough stone walls. The cosy sitting room's primrose yellow sofas are made for flopping into, and on cool evenings logs smoulder in the huge fireplace. A glass or two of what does you good may be proffered by your hosts. Why not sneak into the library for a little contemplation? Perhaps listen to a little light aria (there's a sizeable collection of CDs). Bedrooms extend the pleasing homeliness, while windows frame peaks rising above a vista of firs and forests.

Love time	Top-floor rooms capitalise on the panorama: curl up cosily in an antique wrought-iron bed with rafters above. Some also have old washstands.
Love bites	Join fellow guests for sociable and delicious breakfasts around a long table.
Love it up	Heed the call of nature: trek into the wild Laga Mountains National Park, saddle up, or even swoop over the hills hanggliding.

Bellissimo! The sweet life and mountain spectacle.

Park Hotel Villa Grazioli
Via Umberto Pavoni 19
00046 Grottaferrata, Rome
T +39 069 454 001
F +39 069 413 506
E info@villagrazioli.com
W villagrazioli.com
Francesco Ceribelli
58 rooms and suites
Rates €228-320
Dinner from €80

Open all year round

Extras

Courtesy of
Room for Romance:
A complimentary bottle of
prosecco in your room.

Airport

Rome Ciampino (10 km)
Rome Fiumicino (35 km)

Arrival

From Rome: take ring
road east (direction
Naples) to Junction 21,
signed Frascati. Follow
signs to Piazza Marconi
in Frascati and then follow
hotel signs.

Park Hotel Villa Grazioli

The nobles of Renaissance Rome certainly knew how to live. They also knew just where to escape from the Eternally busy city – which is how Villa Grazioli came to be built in rolling countryside not far away. There's something very dramatic about the way the villa sits atop Frascati's Tuscolo Hills, with its commanding views of Rome, 12 miles distant. Within lie more marvels: room after room overlaid with ravishing frescoes and paintings, trompe l'oeil and decorative plasterwork. Gaze up and be spellbound: unicorns leap, eagles soar, lions pounce and cherubs flutter in a series of lavishly painted vaulted ceilings. This former 16th century cardinal's residence glories in vast salons, halls and galleries with polished marble and tiled floors, fine old furniture and portraits of nobility. It's no museum though; enjoyment courses through the panoramic terraces, the Aquaviva restaurant with its artfully presented Mediterranean cuisine, and the acres of parkland. Tables spill out into the canopied gardens on warm nights, letting guests dine by candleglow. It's just the place to quaff a bottle of the area's famous white wine.

Love time	Get ready for luxury: boudoirs boast sumptuous fabrics and antiques.
Love bites	Be tempted by duck with pear and Chianti, or swordfish with pureed leeks.
Love it up	Try cookery classes and wine tastings; discover Renaissance monuments and sites; swim, play golf, or take parkland strolls.

Bellissimo! ► Cardinal's villa, dramatically blessed.

SARDINIA

Porto Torres
Olbia
218
Sassari
Alghero
S131
S131
Nuoro
Oliena
220
Oristano
Cagliari

LOVE IT If you're after a sophisticated sea-and-sunshine holiday mix, then it has to be Sardinia. The island's uncrowded beaches, clear seas and backdrop of rugged mountains make it a great choice for laidback, outdoorsy holidays. **When to go** Come in summer to make the most of the Mediterranean climate. **Don't miss** The Costa Smeralda's chic resorts: dip into Porto Cervo's maze of alleyways or Porto Rafael's sleepy piazzas and yacht club. Climb one of the old Spanish watchtowers dotting the coastline and clock the views across to the Maddelena islands, or head for the diving mecca of Cannigione, sheltered near the Gulf of Arzachena; a great place for a bike ride. Sardinia is not a culture-free zone, either. There are Roman relics to uncover, and it's worth climbing the spiral stairs to the octagonal bell tower of Alghero's imposing cathedral. **Dine on** Wild boar and suckling pig in the mountains, or lobster, octopus and clam soup by the shore. **Drink up** You can't go wrong with Sardinian wine labels like Vermentino and Canonau. Knock back a Mirto after dinner – a chaser made from myrtle leaves.

THE SEA-AND-SUN COMBO

Pages 218-221

Ca' La Somara
Località Sarra Balestra
07021 Arzachena
T/F +39 0789 98969
E calasomara@tiscali.it
W calasomara.it
Alberto Lagatolla
8 rooms
Rates €70-136
Dinner from €40

Extras Courtesy of
Room for Romance:
Fresh flowers or basket
of fresh fruit in your
room.

Airport Olbia (20 km)

Arrival From Olbia: follow the
S125 north towards
Arzachena and you will
see the hotel signposted.

Closed late Nov – late Feb

Ca' La Somara

Soak up the vibes of the Costa Smeralda without the noisy glitz and glamour. This modest farmhouse, two miles from the famed emerald seas and white sands, is a rural retreat to seduce the senses. Owners Alberto and Laura escaped the rat race to come here; they know what it takes to ensure you unwind. There are hammocks on your porch, big stripey cushions to flop on, a semi-wild garden and an organic shaped pool. Rooms are in the converted stables, a low rise, whitewashed building surrounding a courtyard. Jade green doors, custard yellow borders, massed geraniums, fig trees and cacti, and the odd farm implement add breezy touches. Inside, all is cool and simple: white walls, raftered ceilings, tiled floors and clean-lined, wooden furniture. Love the details: embroidered bedspreads, oil lamps, a niche with a coloured pot, an alcove with an armchair. Splashes of copper, gold, silver and pink add warmth while bathrooms are bright with hand painted tiles. People-watch from La Pergola's bar in starry Porto Cervo then return to the simple pleasures of good food, candlelight and the two of you.

Love time	Bedrooms just as they ought to be: no TVs, no phones, no distractions.
Love bites	Try delicious veggie dishes and desserts, or throw a steak on the barbie.
Love it up	Goggle at the glitzy yachts at Porto Cervo, pack your swimmies for the beach, pedal off on a cycle trail or make friends with the donkeys outside.

Bellissimo! Rural island retreat away from the bright lights.

Su Gologone
Località Su Gologone
08025 Oliena
T +39 0784 287 512
F +39 0784 287 668
E gologone@tin.it
W sugologone.it
Luigi Crisponi
68 rooms
Rates €140-430
Dinner from €70

Airport   Alghero (100 km)

Arrival   From Alghero: take the
S131 then go left on the
S129 and follow signs to
Oliena. The hotel is
signed from there.

Closed November – March

Su Gologone

Sardinia's characteristic scents of rosemary and myrtle seem to surround Su Gologone, an enclave in the heart of the country hidden by olive groves and vineyards. In the distance rise the dramatically jagged peaks of the Supramonte of Oliena. It's the sort of setting you can't fail to be smitten by, nor the atmospheric comforts of the hotel itself. Reception rooms are graced by artisanal pieces, pictures and curios – all chosen with skill. Likewise the restaurant, where gleaming copper pans cling to walls and vast hams dangle from the ceiling. And let's not forget the cavernous cellar, with its bulging casks and vats, nor the library with its intriguing bibliographical ephemera – borrow a book to curl up on the quiet little terraces that intersperse the buildings. The dining terrace is particularly pretty, framed by cascades of flowers and overlooking the pool and jacuzzi – both fed by spring water. The sea isn't far away, and a health and beauty centre ensures guests are kept in shape. After all, if Su Gologone looks this good, why not you?

Love time	Beamed rooms are tastefully done up in shades of sunshine yellow.
Love bites	Delectable regional cuisine includes suckling pig roasted on the spit before you, washed down with the island's own Cannoneau vintages.
Love it up	Gorges, valleys, lunar landscapes, craggy coasts and ancient sites await. Try hiking, quad biking, a four-wheel drive safari or some spa treatments.
Bellissimo	Country living with class, Sardinian style.

NAPLES & THE AMALFI COAST

LOVE IT Towering cliffs, towns tumbling down into the sea, views to die for... this is Italy at its spectacular best. Yesterday's literati and today's glitterati flock to this region, set in the midst of Campania. **When to go** Avoid midsummer crowds (and traffic) and come early or late. **Don't miss** Glamorous Capri, picture-perfect Positano and lofty Ravello, floating 1,000 feet up on a clifftop. Take a heart-thumping ride along the spectacular Amalfi coastal road, carved into a vertiginous cliffside; see an open-air concert at Ravello's Villa Rufolo; check out Mount Vesuvius and Pompeii; take a boat ride along the coast. Top and tail your trip in Naples, with its art museums, Italianate squares and narrow-laned *centro storico*. See the Cilento national park and Paestum beaches from Salerno. **Dine on** Naples is the home of calzone (stuffed pizza), while fresh seafood – clams, squid and octopus – can't be bettered along the coast. **Drink up** You'll need to refuel with an ice-cold limoncello after tackling the hairy Amalfi coast drive. Local nectars also include some fine Caserta wines.

ROMANCE ON A CLIFFTOP

Pages 224-259

Costantinopoli 104
Via Santa Maria di Costantinopoli 104
80138 Naples
T +39 081 557 1035
F +39 081 557 1051
E info@costantinopoli104.it
W costantinopoli104.it
Clelia Santoro
19 rooms
Rates €200-240

Open all year round

Extras

Courtesy of
Room for Romance:
Fresh flowers and a bottle
of champagne in your
room.

Airport   Naples (12 km)

Arrival   From Naples Airport:
transfers arranged.
The hotel is close to
Piazza Bellini in the old
part of Naples. Nearest
metro station: Piazza
Dante.

Costantinopoli 104

This captivating little 19th century villa hides its charms behind a gated courtyard in the heart of old Naples. Leaving behind the city's chaotic streetlife, with its *motorini* (mopeds), lines of washing and fading classical palazzi, we suddenly stepped into a secluded courtyard shaded by lofty palms, where the sounds of the city seemed a million miles away. The Costantinopoli feels like a rich friend's stylish Neapolitan mansion. A huge Liberty style stained glass window in bright jewel colours sets off the facade, with its pretty café-style terrace, while inside everything has been beautifully pulled together by owner Clelia Santoro. Cream sofas stuffed with plump cushions, cool tiled floors and oriental kilims are set off by striking artworks, tall vases of fresh flowers and collections of old prints. Our room came with a wrought iron bed and marble bathroom stocked with designer toiletries. After a hard day's sightseeing, a twilight dip in the guitar-shaped pool hit the spot before sipping a glass of the hotel's home-distilled limoncello.

Love time   A fabulous duplex suite showcases bold pieces of modern art, a
              four-poster in bleached oak and deep mosaic-tiled whirlpool bath for two.
Love bites   Munch delicious breakfasts al fresco on the courtyard terrace.
Love it up   Gorge on the art of Caravaggio, Titian and Michelangelo at the Museo di
              Capodimonte, or head for the Bay of Naples and its islands.

Bellissimo!▶   Elegant Neapolitan mansion run with pizazz.

Grand Hotel Parker's
Corso Vittorio Emanuele 135
80121 Naples
T +39 081 761 2474
F +39 081 663 527
E info@grandhotelparkers.it
W grandhotelparkers.com
Vittorio Morelli
82 rooms
Rates €200-360
Dinner from €160

Open all year round

Extras Courtesy of
Room for Romance:
A special gift in your room
– pastries or ceramics.

Airport Naples (11 km)

Arrival From Naples Airport: take
the tangenziale (ring road)
to exit 9, signed Vomero.
Follow directions to Via
Cilea/Via Tasso. Turn left
at end of street into Corso
Vittorio Emanuele. Valet
parking.

Grand Hotel Parker's

Overlooking the sweeping Bay of Naples from a lofty avenue lined with palms, Grand Hotel Parker's has all the grandeur you would expect of a hotel with a long and illustrious past. Its star-studded roll-call of guests over the years runs from Oscar Wilde and Clark Gable to rock stars escaping today's paparazzi. Proud of its historic British links – the hotel was named after one George Parker Bidder, who made it his home for nearly 20 years in the 1880s – it offers an unadulterated taste of genteel living. Art and antiques set the tone in the marbled lobby, while elegant, spacious rooms are suitably restrained, with soothing shades, classic dark wood and swish bathrooms. You can recharge your batteries with a menu of treatments in the hotel's up-to-the-minute day spa, but we'd say the pièce de résistance at this Neapolitan grande dame is George's top-floor restaurant, whose terrific terrace is flanked by bronze torch-bearing nymphs. With wines from the owner's own estate, this is definitely one of the city's don't-miss dining spots.

Love time   For real indulgence. retire to a lavishly refurbished split-level suite.
Love bites   Flirt by candlelight over cocktails on the terrace before dining with Naples twinkling at your feet. Chef Vincenzo Baciot gives cooking plenty of pizazz.
Love it up   You're just a short cab ride away from the city's top museums and galleries, and minutes from the boats speeding to Ischia and Capri.

Bellissimo!   Park yourselves here for grand nights in Naples.

Mezzatorre Resort & Spa
Via Mezzatorre 23
80075 Forio d'Ischia
T +39 081 986 111
F +39 081 986 015
E info@mezzatorre.it
W mezzatorre.it
Giovanni Sirabella
52 rooms, 9 suites
Rates €250-2,500
Dinner from €75

Open April – October

Extras   Courtesy of
                Room for Romance:
                A complimentary chilled
                bottle of champagne in
                your room.

Airport   Naples (40 km)

Arrival   From Naples Airport: take
                taxi or ANM bus to Naples
                harbour for ferry or
                hydrofoil to Isle of Ischia,
                where hotel will arrange
                pick-up. Use the hotel's
                official taxis while in Ischia.

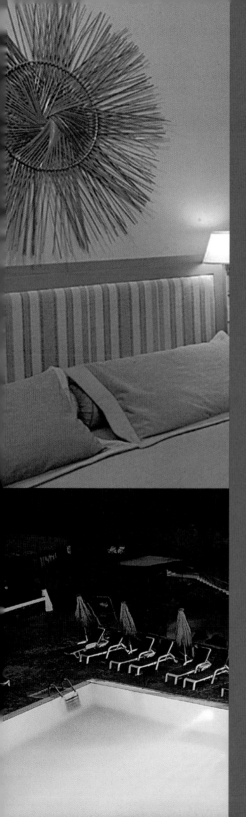

Mezzatorre Resort & Spa

Spread over a promontory overlooking the Bay of Naples, this five-star island hideaway could have escaped from a movie set. Film lovers will be inspired by the famous director Luchino Visconti's former villa within the oak and pine dappled grounds. Forget Death in Venice; this intimate haven of pleasure will make you feel you've arrived in heaven. The focal point is a beautifully restored 15th century Saracen watchtower. Moorish archways invite you inside to elegant sitting rooms and bedrooms with dazzling Med views. Scattered among the pine groves are luxurious, more spacious rooms – ours was all warm coral tones and cool blues with classic Neapolitan Majolica tiles and marble. Get steamy in the bubbling thermal waters of the spa and beauty centre, or messy smeared with the famous volcanic Ischian mud. Submit to expert therapists' hands and emerge rejuvenated and glossy, in touch with your inner selves.We loved the warm cliff-edge seawater pool, with its private rocky beach below. A hotel with a blissful setting.

Love time   Open plan suites have private gardens and whirlpools – very back to nature.
Love bites   Dine al fresco under a palm-leaf roof in the poolside restaurant. The aptly named Panoramic Restaurant serves gourmet dishes on candlelit terraces.
Love it up   Stroll up to the rugged promontory Il Pensatoio, with no-one but seagulls for company. Capri and the Amalfi coast are just a speedboat zip away.

Bellissimo! ▶   Ischia's heaven on earth.

Capri Palace Hotel & Spa
Via Capodimonte
80071 Anacapri
T +39 081 978 0111
F +39 081 837 3191
E info@capri-palace.com
W capri-palace.com
Ermanno Zanini
67 rooms, 13 suites
Rates €295-2,600
Dinner from €190

Closed November – early April

Extras	Courtesy of Room for Romance: A bottle of chilled sparkling wine in your room.
Airport	Naples (55 km)
Arrival	From Naples Airport: take a taxi or ANM bus to Naples port for the hydrofoil or ferry to Capri. The hotel will arrange a pick-up from the quayside.

Capri Palace

Life doesn't get much ritzier than at the Capri Palace. This temple of conspicuous wealth boasts superlative views of the Bay of Naples, utterly fabulous interiors and reams of A-list celebrity guests (Harrison Ford, Julia Roberts and Mariah Carey if you love to name-drop). A phalanx of slick staff – all impeccably designer-suited – are clearly used to handling divas as well as dreamers. Follow the serpentine path lined with billowing muslin up from Anacapri's square and you're suddenly on another planet. Everything is done out in cool, expensive ivory with sprawling sofas, huge burnished gold mirrors, towering candelabra and audacious modern artworks. Vaulted ceilings and colonnades perfectly set off the bold mix of modern design and Louis XVI antiques, while decadent marble bathrooms are equally statement-making. Our junior suite, brilliantly toned in shades of cream and cappuccino, had a Berber style tented bed and vast terrace. The outdoor pool is heated (naturally) and the beauty farm is just the place to indulge – if your plastic can take the pace.

Love time	The rooftop Megaron suite, with its own private pool, is swoon-worthy.
Love bites	Vanilla candles, petals and lemon trees make L'Olivo, owner of Capri's only Michelin star, a dreamy setting for dinner. Dig into dishes such as red shrimp with burrato cheese and caviar on asparagus and apple salad.
Love it up	People-watch in the bar, or step aboard one of the hotel's private yachts.

Bellissimo! *La dolce vita* doesn't get more chic than this.

Grand Hotel Excelsior Vittoria
Piazza Tasso 34
80067 Sorrento
T +39 081 807 1044
F +39 081 877 1206
E exvitt@exvitt.it
W excelsiorvittoria.com
Paolo Sanavia
98 rooms and suites
Rates €390-2,100
Dinner from €110

Open all year round

Extras
Courtesy of
Room for Romance:
Welcome drink on arrival,
plus welcome gift and fruit
basket in your room.

Airport Naples (50 km)

Arrival
From Naples: take the A3
towards Salerno, then
SS145 for Sorrento. Head
for Piazza Tasso in the
town centre and you will
see the hotel gates. Valet
parking.

Hotel Excelsior Vittoria

This clifftop grande dame majestically surveying Mount Vesuvius and the Bay of Naples has played host to a chocolate-box of big names over the years. Dating back to the early 1800s and reached through five acres of lush gardens lined with orange and lemon groves, it offers an extravagant taste of old-time romance in a sumptuous Mediterranean setting. Elegant salons are set off with classical and Belle Epoque flourishes, from the Liberty style winter garden to the turn-of-the-century music room, where you can imagine Victorian ladies flirtatiously playing the coquette. Rooms and suites cater for every comfort, with most having a balcony or terrace. Lavishly domed frescoed ceilings, gilded mirrors and soft lighting make the Vittoria restaurant a shamelessly romantic setting to sample some of chef Vincenzo Galano's award-winning Neapolitan cuisine. There's a touch of the tropics in the Trani marble pool shaded by orange trees, and a private lift down to the harbour should you fancy zipping off in a boat.

Love time Splurge on one of the opulent suites if you dare; we loved the Vittoria, whose large terrace begs for champagne and a technicolour sunset.

Love bites Dine al fresco beneath white sails by the pool; sip champers on the Bosquet terrace or go the full Monty with dinner in the lavish Vittoria.

Love it up Sorrento's shops and café-lined streets await outside the gates.

Bellissimo! ▶ Belle Epoque beauty in lush Sorrento setting.

Maison La Minervetta
Via Capo 25
80067 Sorrento
T +39 081 877 4455
F +39 081 878 4601
E info@laminervetta.com
W laminervetta.com
Eugenia Di Leva
12 rooms
Rates €250-350

Extras Courtesy of
Room for Romance:
Room upgrade to next
available class.

Airport Naples (60 km)

Arrival From Naples: take the A3
towards Salerno and
SS145 to Sorrento. The
hotel is just past the town
centre on the right.

Closed 1 November – 1 March

Maison La Minervetta

Step inside this white-walled 1950s villa on Sorrento's cliffside and you could have walked straight into the pages of an interior design magazine. Architect Marco de Luca has created a stunning contemporary address that feels more like an airy Mediterranean style loft apartment than a conventional hotel. All is glass and light, with floor-to-ceiling windows capturing stunning Bay of Naples views at every turn. The vibrant colours of the South give La Minervetta immense visual vrooom, set off by sleek modern furniture and smart lighting. Deep turquoise is strikingly teamed with navy and lime green; orange is played up to the hilt with coral red and yellow; reds and whites contrast with stripes of darkest blue. There's no pared-down minimalism here; walls are set off by flamboyant artworks and collections of ceramics and pottery from around the world, all brilliantly presented in trademark alcoves or miniature shelves. Retro '60s armchairs and lampshades lend a classic edge while a series of still-lifes – a line of pebbles, a bowl of shells or an artful arrangement of twigs – provide endless fascination. We were smitten.

Love time   Every room is a winner here, though our fave was number 8, with its wrap-around glass where only the waves can watch you.

Love bites   Cooked breakfasts are served family-style in the chequerboard-tiled kitchen.

Love it up   Gaze at Mount Vesuvius, or head to the hotel's slice of private beach.

Bellissimo!   Plum designer address bursting with Wow factor.

Oasi Olimpia Relais
Via Deserto 26
80064 Sant'Agata Sui Due Golfi
T +39 081 808 0560
F +39 081 808 5214
E info@oasiolimpiarelais.it
W oasiolimpiarelais.it
Carmen Mazzola
12 rooms
Rates €210-775
Dinner from €130

Closed 15 November – 1 March

Extras

Courtesy of
Room for Romance:
A welcome dinner and
a bottle of wine in your
room.

Airport   Naples (68 km)

Arrival   From Naples: take the A3
towards Salerno then the
SS145 to Sorrento. Follow
the Positano road at Meta.
Turn off for Sant'Agata
Sui Due Golfi. Hotel
signed on entering village.

Oasi Olimpia Relais

Set above the village of Sant'Agata Sui Due Golfi on the spine of the Sorrento Peninsula (shades of Ravello in this lofty hilltop enclave with its sweeping views), this beautifully managed hotel is an unexpected find. You'll need a car to stay here – it's a 20-minute drive up past olive and lemon groves from Sorrento – but it's just the place to escape the holiday crowds. Built in 1892 by a German aristocrat, the villa retains heaps of original features and visual appeal. Rooms are attractively furnished with tiled floors, cream walls, starched lace curtains and carved wooden bedsteads. Some have a small terrace, while the four junior suites have a sitting room and hydro-massage bath. There's some interesting motor racing memorabilia around, and you can even go for a spin in the owner's vintage Alfa Romeo Spider or swoop over the Amalfi coast in a helicopter. Rolling grounds with a beautifully secluded pool are just the place for afternoon siestas. Some guests decide to join one of manager Carmen Mazzola's cookery courses; others simply come for a pampering by the incredibly charming staff.

Love time   We loved the terraced penthouse suite: drink in views of Vesuvius and the twin bays of Naples and Salerno from your private outdoor hot tub.

Love bites   Feast on delicious Mediterranean fare in the softly candlelit dining room.

Love it up   Sail along the coast in a traditional Gozzi, with a picnic and champers.

Bellissimo!   Hilltop seclusion in a movie-star setting.

Casa Albertina
Via della Tavolozza 3
84017 Positano
T +39 089 875 143
F +39 089 811 540
E info@casalbertina.il
W casalbertina.it
Lorenzo Cinque
20 rooms
Rates €170-220
Dinner from €50

Open all year round

Extras Courtesy of
Room for Romance:
A complimentary bottle of
Ferrari sparkling wine in
your room.

Airport Naples (60 km)

Arrival From Naples: take A3
south; exit at Castellamare
di Stabia then take SS145
and SS163 to Positano.
Alternatively leave the car
behind and take hydrofoil
direct to Positano.

Casa Albertina

Positano's sugar almond-coloured houses balance like a display of Ferrero Rocher chocolates; remove one and they'd all topple into the sea. Albergo Casa Albertina is perched high among the top layers with staggering views over the rooftops cascading below into the Gulf of Salerno. It's arguably one of the town's top viewpoints and a serenely peaceful location – even if it's a steep, stepped climb to the front door. Small and low-key, it has a charming, old-fashioned elegance well away from the town's tourist-honeypot heart. Cool, white walls, stone archways, acres of Majolica floor tiles and ferns in terracotta pots give it a welcoming, homely feel while pretty painted doors open into simple but gracious bedrooms, in rich reds or Mediterranean blues. Once we found the two terracotta-tiled terraces, with their mesmerising views, we could have happily stayed put. There's nothing pretentious or extravagant about this place, and that's the attraction. Owner Lorenzo Cinque sweeps you up with Italian warmth and, together with his young staff, creates a beguilingly relaxed atmosphere.

Love time   Pretty flowers, marbled bathrooms and breakfast on your private balcony.
Love bites   Traditional Neapolitan dishes – including home-made pasta and Lorenzo's speciality seared tuna – are served in the nicely rustic dining room.
Love it up   Wander among the cute houses and slick boutiques of Positano.

Bellissimo! ➤   Much higher and you'd be up in the clouds.

Eden Roc Suites
Via G. Marconi 110
84017 Positano
T +39 089 875 844
F +39 089 875 552
E info@edenroc.it
W edenroc.it
Raffaele Casola
25 rooms
Rates €198-550
Dinner from €80

Closed 6 November – 28 February

Extras Courtesy of
Room for Romance:
A complimentary chilled
bottle of champagne in
your room.

Airport Naples (60 km)

Arrival From Naples: take the A3
towards Salerno, then
follow directions for
Positano. The hotel is on
your left as you enter the
town, just before road
continues to Amalfi.

Eden Roc Suites

Owned by one of the oldest families in Positano, touches of luxury from marble stairs to silky linens add a touch of Eden to the traditional architecture of this clifftop hotel. Crisp white walls and the purple splash of bougainvillea perfectly complement the soft sage and olive greens of the surrounding landscape, picked up inside by the furnishings. The sirens of mythology were said to sing from the Isole di Galli, specks of rock in the Tyrrhenian Sea laid out hundreds of feet below the famous Amalfi coastal drive, just minutes away. From your private terrace or the scenic rooftop pool, Positano's rooftops tumble away into the cobalt blue sea. Rooms are light, bright and airy, with cool ceramic tiled floors, graceful arches, detailed ceilings, the furniture modern and built for comfort. Bathrooms are a treat, all big with whirlpool baths and jazzy locally painted tiles. At night, sip a cocktail in the American bar and watch from the roof as the lights of Positano and Praiano garland the darkening sea.

Love time   Go for one of the newly refurbished deluxe rooms; the best has a naughty open-air hot tub for two on its private terrace.

Love bites   Dine on traditional Campanian dishes in the Adamo e Eva (need we translate?) restaurant, done out in dusky pinks and ivory.

Love it up   Explore Positano's streets, then get bubbly with a glass of fizz on the roof.

Bellissimo! ▸   Roc-solid address in pretty Positano.

Le Sirenuse
Via Cristoforo Colombo 30
84017 Positano
T +39 089 875 066
F +39 089 811 798
E info@sirenuse.it
W sirenuse.it
Antonio Sersale
61 rooms, 2 suites
Rates €300-850
Dinner from €85

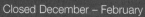

Closed December – February

Extras Courtesy of
Room for Romance:
A complimentary bottle
of Italian sparkling wine
in your room.

Airport Naples (60 km)

Arrival From Naples: take the A3
Salerno highway and exit
at the SS145 Meta di
Sorrento road. Take the
SS163 to Positano. Valet
parking.

Le Sirenuse

For those in the know, this is THE glam place to stay on the Amalfi coast. Achingly chic and regularly showered in awards, Le Sirenuse has played host to scores of celebs over the years. This one-time 18th century palace – former summer residence of owners the Sersale family – has all the feel of an opulent family home. Rooms – all different – come in cool summertime creams, with polished Majolica tile floors. The best have dreamy terraces, views to die for, acres of space and gorgeous toiletries. Suites have decadent jacuzzi baths big enough for a Roman orgy, while flamboyant touches include murals, Asian antiques and fabulously ornate mirrors. Guests can tap into a library of more than 500 DVDs, though with jaw-dropping views of Positano tumbling into the blue Med, you'll feel you're in the front row of the movies anyway. Be pummelled and pampered in the hotel's Aveda spa before languishing by the pool. Or simply slip upstairs to the champagne bar for a nightcap under the stars. Honeymoon heaven starts here.

Love time   Splash out if you dare: sink into a jacuzzi overlooking the sea in one of the Special junior suites.

Love bites   Dine at La Sponda restaurant, lit by candle trees and lulled by mandolins.

Love it up   How about a sunset excursion along the Amalfi coast in the hotel's own boat? Champagne included, naturally.

Bellissimo!   Definitely a place to bliss out.

Hotel Tramonto d'Oro
Via Gennaro Capriglione 119
84010 Praiano
T +39 089 874 955
F +39 089 874 670
E info@tramontodoro.it
W tramontodoro.it
The Esposito family
40 rooms
Rates €180-260
Dinner from €80

Open all year round

Extras Courtesy of
Room for Romance:
One night stay: a bottle of
local red wine. Two nights
plus: a hand-painted
ceramic plate.

Airport Naples (65 km)

Arrival From Naples: Follow
signs for Sorrento and
Positano. Praiano is a
further 5 km. Hotel is on
the right, after a tunnel.

Tramonto d'Oro

From your bedroom, gaze over the Gulf of Salerno to the Siren rocks, legendary home of the temptress mermaids – they sang so sweetly, many a sailor was lured to his death – and you'll be smitten. It's impossible not to fall in love with the Amalfi coast – vertiginous cliffs, turquoise waters – and this hotel, slipped between Positano and Amalfi, has a peach position. Run by the Esposito family for over 50 years, it's built into the cliff face in typical Mediterranean style – cool white walls, Moorish arches, elegant balconies and Majolica floor tiles. Bedrooms are cool and airy with sleek, honey-brown wood furnishings, sunny coloured fabrics and bathrooms prettily tricked out with hand-painted ceramic tiles. Wherever you wander – the roof-top swimming pool, the breakfast terrace, the arch windowed dining room – the views mesmerise. Across the bay lies Positano, cascading down the cliffs; shimmering out at sea is curvaceous Capri; within touching distance are the tower and dome of Praiano's church. The village is small and charming, the Espositos cosset you like family, the sunsets are to die for.

Love time	Deluxe rooms have the largest terraces, and some have jacuzzis.
Love bites	Enjoy fab home cooking. Head waiter Pasquale will adore you, and you him.
Love it up	Take the Sentiero degli Dei (Path of the Gods) for an exhilarating walk to Positano. Cool off afterwards in the roof-top pool, or slip into the sea.

Bellissimo! ▶ Cliffside charmer with ravishing views.

Hotel Santa Caterina
SS Amalfitana 9
84011 Amalfi
T +39 089 871 012
F +39 089 871 351
E info@hotelsantacaterina.it
W hotelsantacaterina.it
Armando di Palma
38 rooms, 24 suites
Rates €250-1,200
Dinner from €50

Open all year round

Extras Courtesy of
Room for Romance:
Flowers, basket of fresh
fruit and cookies in your
room.

Airport Naples (60 km)

Arrival From Naples: take the A3
highway towards Salerno.
Exit for Vietri sul Mare and
follow signs for Amalfi. Go
through the town towards
Positano; hotel is on left.
Valet parking.

Santa Caterina

Few places are made for *amore* like the Santa Caterina, a dazzling white wedding cake of a hotel perched on the side of a cliff with a grandstand view of the Bay of Amalfi. Brad and Angelina and a host of other Hollywood celebs have pulled down the shutters of its sumptuous suites, where only the rustle of the orange groves disturbs the peace. Huge full-length windows in the lounge look out onto a spectacular terrace dripping with bougainvillea, below which cliffs plunge dramatically down to the sea. Terraced gardens tumble down to the saltwater pool far below, from where you can dip into the Tyrrhenian Sea. Knockout surroundings are only part of this grand, early 20th century hotel's appeal. Bedrooms are creamy and luxurious, while bathrooms with extravagantly muralled walls and (in some) glass domed ceilings have all the treats you would expect – bubbly jacuzzi baths, outsize showers and heaps of lotions and potions. For the max in hideaway heaven, book one of the three deliciously private lovers' lairs in the grounds.

Love time No plans to surface? Suites made for round-the-clock lurve include the Follia Amalfitana, complete with vast bed, private terrace with uninterrupted views of the sea and a sunken jacuzzi.

Love bites Dine poolside or in the smart terrace restaurant, where the seafood is A1.

Love it up The fabled Amalfi coast is right outside the door; the town's at your feet.

Bellissimo! ❥ Top-drawer address made for love nesters.

Hotel Caruso
Piazza San Giovanni del Toro 2
Ravello 84010
T +39 089 858 801
F +39 089 858 806
E reservations@hotelcaruso.net
W hotelcaruso.com
Giampaolo Ottazzi
52 rooms
Rates €668-817, suites €994-2,420
Dinner from €200

Closed November – March

Extras Courtesy of
Room for Romance:
A complimentary chilled
bottle of sparkling wine in
your room.

Airport Naples (64 km)

Arrival From Naples: take the A3
south, exit at Valico di
Chiunzi and follow signs
to Ravello. Valet parking.

Hotel Caruso

If nothing but the swishest, plushest and most extravagant address will do, then it has to be the Caruso. Built as a palace in the 11th century, this place has been Ravello's most famous address since it first opened in 1893. Greta Garbo, Jackie Kennedy, Humphrey Bogart and a line of other celebs have all stayed. Now completely renovated by the Orient Express group, the new-look Caruso – just out of wrappers – combines five-star elegance with those knockout 360-degree Ravello views. Several magnificent frescoed ceilings have been uncovered during the two-year refurbishment. A terrace with Norman arches and sumptuous furnishings frames the gardens, filled with pergolas, oleanders and wisteria, and guarded by stone lions. The separate Belvedere has seven suites with an enormous garden as well as a terrace, while the spa offers an array of pampering treatments. Soak up the views at the stunning cliff-edge infinity pool, before sipping cocktails (the barman mixes a mean bellini) and dining beneath starry skies on the Belvedere terrace.

Love time   Lock yourselves in the Jackie O suite, with its terrace and private pool.
Love bites   Book a ringside seat on the Belvedere terrace, with the lights of the *costiera Amalfitana* twinkling far below, to enjoy classic Italian cuisine.
Love it up   Set sail on the hotel's own boat, visit the ruins of Pompeii and Paestum, or get tickets for an open-air classical concert at Ravello's Villa Rufolo.

Bellissimo!   The high life starts here – assuming you can flash the cash.

Palazzo Sasso
Via San Giovanni del Toro 28
84010 Ravello
T +39 089 818 181
F +39 089 858 900
E info@palazzosasso.com
W palazzosasso.com
Stefano Gegnacorsi
31 rooms, 12 suites
Rates €300-2,000
Dinner from €200

Closed November – March

Extras Courtesy of
Room for Romance:
A complimentary chilled
bottle of prosecco in your
room.

Airport Naples (70 km)

Arrival From Naples: exit the A3
Salerno highway at Angri
and follow signs to Costa
Amalfitana and Ravello.
Call the hotel and a porter
will be in the square to
collect your bags.

Palazzo Sasso

This sugar-pink palace with mesmeric clifftop views over the vertiginous Amalfi coast is a place to turn on the glitz. Polished marble mosaic floors and equally polished staff set the tone in the lavish lobby guarded by stone mermaids, marble lions and torch-bearing nymphs, while immaculate staff are tuned into the demands of high-maintenance guests. Elegant sofas and flamboyant artworks line the lounge and piano bar while outside, lofty palms flutter over terraces beckoning for cocktails. Rooms are as sumptuous as you would expect, with creamy-light furniture, hand-made Vietri tiles, dazzling marble and gleaming gold and brass fittings. Guests can even choose from a menu of Frette bedlinen, sliding into king-size beds dressed in linen, satin or soft cotton sheets. The extravagant cliff-side pool with its fountains and manicured terraces is the perfect place to loll away an afternoon, while a glass-walled lift will whisk you up to the rooftop whirlpools. The Sasso's two Michelin star restaurant Rossellini's (named after Ingrid Bergman, who stayed here with movie mogul Roberto Rossellini back in the 1940s), is one of the region's best.

Love time   Ready to splurge big-time? Try the breathtaking terraced Belvedere suite.
Love bites   Don't miss a starlit dinner at Rossellini's – an all-evening gastronomic affair where each course is to be savoured.
Love it up   Explore Ravello's lush gardens or simply chill – do you really want to stir?

Bellissimo!   Sumptuous living at highbrow clifftop palace.

Villa Cimbrone
Via Santa Chiara 26
84010 Ravello
T +39 089 857 459
F +39 089 857 777
E info@villacimbrone.com
W villacimbrone.com
Paola Vuilleumier
19 rooms
Rates €330-715
Dinner from €60

Closed 15 November – 31 March

Extras Courtesy of
Room for Romance:
A chilled bottle of
prosecco and fruit basket
in your room.

Airport Naples (70 km)

Arrival From Naples: exit the A3
Salerno highway at Angri
and follow signs to Costa
Amalfitana and Ravello.
Park off main square; call
hotel and a porter will
meet you (10 mins walk).

Villa Cimbrone

Arriving at Villa Cimbrone is rather like walking into a living temple of art. We were instantly smitten by its sublime hilltop location, fabulous gardens, extravaganza of artworks and heart-stopping views sweeping down from Ravello to the sea. Temples, gazebos, crumbling cloisters, pillars mantled in vines and dozens of classical statues make it a must for anyone passionate about art. My girlfriend couldn't tear herself away from the Terrazza dell'Infinito, with its row of sun-weathered marble busts and stunning backdrop of the Cilento mountains. The villa itself is bursting with artistic treasures, yet still has the feel of a wealthy friend's historic home. Rooms are strewn with antiques and huge armoires, with the best having frescoed ceilings, huge stone fireplaces and original Majolica tile floors as well as ample old-time comforts. There's a terrific pool terrace framed with cliff-edge views, and you can have the park to yourself at dusk, when visitors are gone. Greta Garbo famously eloped here with her lover Leopold Stokowsky back in the 1930s, and not surprisingly, lovers have been entwining here ever since.

Love time   Our deliciously atmospheric bedroom faced right over the sea, so no need to close the shutters…

Love bites   Ravello's incomparable views make dining on the villa's terrace a must.

Love it up   Palazzi, churches and winding streets await exploration outside the gates.

Bellissimo!   Romance in spades at aristocratic hilltop villa.

Hotel Villa Maria
Via Santa Chiara 2
84010 Ravello
T +39 089 857 255
F +39 089 857 071
E villamaria@villamaria.it
W villamaria.it
Vincenzo Palumbo
23 rooms
Rates €220-440
Dinner from €90

Open all year round

Extras Courtesy of
Room for Romance:
A complimentary bottle of
sparkling wine in your
room.

Airport Naples (70 km)

Arrival From Naples: from the A2
highway join A30 (Caserta
Sud) and follow signs to
Costa Amalfitana and
Ravello. There is no direct
car access to hotel; call
for luggage assistance.

Villa Maria

Lovers just can't stay away from Villa Maria. Clifftop views over the Vallone del Dragone, a fabulous palm-shaded terrace and all the intimacy of a hilltop Italianate villa make it one of Ravello's most sought-after addresses. We met couples who come back here year after year simply because they wouldn't dream of staying anywhere else. The graceful, peach-coloured villa epitomises all of Ravello's charms. There's none of that big-hotel formality, and all the feel of an extravagant private home. Walk inside, and it's all cool marble chequerboard floors, crystal chandeliers and mellow family antiques. Bedrooms are furnished with old-fashioned brass beds and antiques, while some freshly remodelled bathrooms have deep jacuzzi tubs. Guests can laze by the pool of the nearby Hotel Giordano – also owned by the Palumbo family – and hospitable staff add to the charm. Dining on the much-lauded restaurant terrace, with those heart-thumping Ravello vistas, is not to be missed. Lanterns glow from the fig trees, and with the valley lights twinkling way below this is an unbeatable place to while away an evening. And so to bed...

Love time	The palatial first floor suite has a hand-carved armoire, and vast terrace.
Love bites	Expect top-notch cooking using the hotel's own organic produce. The sweet-sharp lemon granita is sensational.
Love it up	Tying the knot? Sister property Villa Eva is the place for a dazzling party.

Bellissimo! Peach of a place bursting with Ravello charm.

Palazzo Belmonte
84072 Santa Maria di Castellabate
Salerno
T +39 0974 960 211
F +39 0974 961 150
E reservations@palazzobelmonte.it
W palazzobelmonte.com
Prince Belmonte
50 rooms
Rates €182-668
Dinner from €108

Closed 31 October – 6 May

Extras

Courtesy of
Room for Romance:
A bottle of sparkling wine
and chocolates in your
room, or room upgrade
subject to availability.

Airport Naples (120 km)

Arrival From Naples: take the A3
to Salerno then SS18 to
Agripoli. Follow signs
to Santa Maria di
Castellabate, from where
the hotel is signposted.

Palazzo Belmonte

Can you have too much of a good thing? Not here, you can't. Take the location of 17th century Palazzo Belmonte: an unspoilt stretch of Campanian coastline nudging the fishing village of Santa Maria di Castellabate. What's more, this is the heart of the Cilento National Park, a UNESCO world heritage site whose surrounding waters have been praised for their environmental excellence. What was once a hunting lodge for the kings of Italy and Spain still looks good, too. Thick walls enclose five acres of landscaping. Within, guests can stay inside the palazzo itself, in Edoardo's House or Villa Belmonte in the grounds. Bougainvillea tumbles down brickwork; gardens rustle with orange and lemon trees, the air further scented with jasmine and rose. A freshwater pool floats in a profusion of greenery, while a secret door leads to a private beach with a stretch of peachy sand. A fine restaurant offers Med-inspired cuisine. Dine at the Belvedere at dusk when it's glowing with torches, candlelight and stardust, with the waves almost lapping at your feet, and it feels almost lyrical.

Love time   Distinctively decorated suites have vaulted ceilings and private terraces.
Love bites   Gaze across the water towards Capri from the torchlit restaurant.
Love it up   Sail along the legendary Amalfi coast; dig around the big archeological sites; take boat trips to unspoilt Punta Licosa or Capri; scuba dive or ride.

Bellissimo!   Dreamy coast-hugging palazzo delivers the works.

Domus Laeta
Via Flavio Gioia
84050 Giungano, Salerno
T +39 0828 880 177
F +39 081 764 5862
E info@domuslaeta.com
W domuslaeta.com
The Aulisio family
8 rooms
Rates €90-110

Extras Courtesy of
Room for Romance:
A bottle of wine in your
room on arrival.

Airport Naples (120 km)

Arrival From Naples: take the
A3 to Salerno, then take
the SS18 and follow
directions for Giungano.

Open all year round

Domus Laeta

Slip through the creeper-covered arched entrance and time stands still. The cool courtyards, lofty windows, rough thick walls and stone-flagged passageways of this fortified village mansion seem little changed since it was built over 300 years ago. One of the oldest houses in Giungano, it stands next to the main square and ancient church. Step inside and you're wrapped in an aura of well-ordered, well-heeled calm. You too can live like an aristocrat in the former home of the noble Aulisio family. Browse a book in the red-walled library, sink into deep sofas in the fire-lit salon, sip an espresso under the frescoes of the airy loggia, dine under the lofty beams of the Grand Hall. Original floor tiles – polished and time-worn – family antiques and oil paintings lend a gracious air. Bedrooms, too, are oases of calm. Their terracotta floors, high ceilings, shuttered windows, elegant country furnishings and pretty bedcovers keep them simple yet utterly comfortable. There's plenty to do in the area but chances are you'll want to linger in the terraced garden or dip into the infinity-style pool, with fabulous views over the Paestum plain.

Love time	Book the Terrazzo room for all-over tanning on the private rooftop terrace.
Love bites	Breakfast is a gourmet buffet, and staff can suggest good local trattorias.
Love it up	Paestum's archaeological sites are the big draw here, but don't ignore the beaches, grottoes of Capo Palinuro and the national Park of Cilento.

Bellissimo! ▶ Hilltop views over a timeless landscape.

PUGLIA

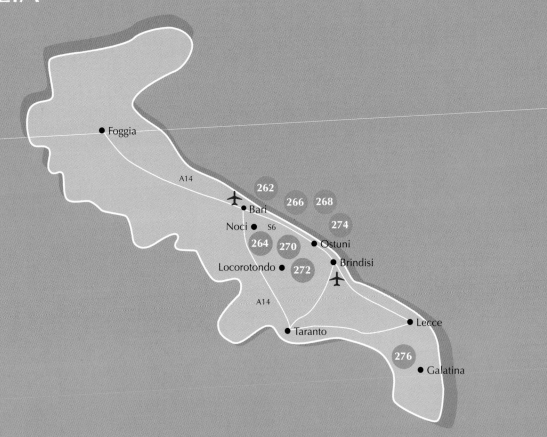

- Foggia
- A14
- 262
- 266 268
- Bari
- 274
- Noci S6
- 264 270
- Ostuni
- Locorotondo
- 272
- Brindisi
- A14
- Taranto
- Lecce
- 276
- Galatina

LOVE IT Miles of grassy dunes and silver-green olive groves, burning white sugar-cube towns, intense turquoise-blue waters... that's Puglia. Washed by the Adriatic on one side and the Ionian Sea on the other, the heel of Italy's boot still remains remarkably untrodden. **When to go** High summer for max tanning, late spring to catch the carpet of flowers. **Don't miss** Wonderful Lecce – the so-called Florence of the Baroque – with its riotously ornate central piazza and narrow lanes. Fortified Ostuni, set on three hills rising over the Adriatic, also begs to be seen. Alberobello and Locorotondo have entire streets of beehive-roofed Trulli homes, while Castellana has underground caves to explore. Immensely stylish hotels have shades of the exotic, with adobe-style architecture and Moroccan flourishes. **Dine on** Puglia is the garden of Italy – the place to enjoy locally made pastas, soft cheeses, olive oils and every kind of fruit. **Drink up** Try one of the potent local wines, or join the locals for an iced coffee with almond syrup – latte di mandorla – while you sit in the sunshine.

DAZZLING SHADES OF THE SOUTH

Pages 262-277

Masseria Serra dell'Isola
Strada Provinciale 165, n. 35
70042 Mola di Bari
T +39 349 531 1256
F +39 080 476 979
E info@masseriaserradellisola.it
W masseriaserradellisola.it
Rita Guastamacchia
6 rooms
Rates €100-120
Dinner from €70

Open all year round

Extras

Airport

Arrival

Courtesy of
Room for Romance:
Biscotti all'anice and *vino liquoroso* in your room.

Bari (25 km)

From Bari: take SS16 (E55) towards Mola. Then go right into via San Onofrio and right again onto Strada Provinciale 165; straight on for 3.5 km and the hotel is on your right.

Masseria Serra dell'Isola

Step through the pillared gateway, under the olive and almond trees and into the arms of this whitewashed masseria. Rita's family have lived here for almost 300 years and there's a tangible sense that little has changed. Fires still burn in the terracotta stoves in the high-vaulted, former olive press – now the living room. Sepia-tinted photographs line the walls, antiques and family heirlooms fill the rooms, copper pans glint in the kitchen. Every room, you feel, has many stories to tell. Named after the women of Rita's family, bedrooms have an unpretentious, country warmth. With white walls, large windows – some with balconies – and polished tile floors, they're furnished with pretty wrought-iron bedsteads, embroidered bedspreads and charming paintings. A collection of jugs, a chaise longue scattered with cushions, and lacy cloths on bedside tables are welcoming details. Borrow a bicycle and explore the countryside, read a book in the shade of a garden tree, savour genuine home cooking. The masseria's simple homeliness will wrap you in its warmth.

Love time   The Donna Ritella room, with its brass four-poster, is pure romance.
Love bites   You'll relish classic Puglian dishes – lamb with seasonal vegetables, chickpeas and calamari, *biancomangiare* (Puglian almond crème caramel).
Love it up   Try Rita's home-made *rosoli* – fruit liquors made to an ancient family recipe. Sip *Elisir d'Amore* and who knows what might happen...

Bellissimo! ▶   Country-cousin charm and warmth.

Abate Masseria and Resort
Strada Provinciale per Massafra km 0,300
70015 Noci
T +39 080 497 8288
F +39 080 497 8023
E info@abatemasseria.it
W abatemasseria.it
Angelica Perta
8 Rooms
Rates €110-186

Open all year round

Extras

Courtesy of
Room for Romance:
A bottle of champagne,
chocolate surprise and
local fruit compote.

Airport   Bari (55 km)

Arrival   From Bari: take A14 (Via
Gioia Del Colle) to Noci.
Continue to Alberobello,
turn right at high school
towards Martina Franca,
then straight on at traffic
lights; signed from there.

Abate Masseria

Gnarled oaks and walnut trees, conical roofs peeping over the walls like a row of clown's hats – you'll wonder where you are. These tiny, creamy-white, round stone buildings that look more like a row of doll's houses are the typical *trulli* homes of Puglia. Origin unknown, here they're part of an ancient farm estate that seems wrapped in a timewarp. An orchard, courtyards, gardens, private corners with a table for two, a tiny white church – it's a story book brought to life. This country simplicity has been subtly modernised without losing its charm. Bedrooms – in the trulli or in the stables – are rustic chic havens of red tiled floors, white plaster and stone walls, white cushions on cane furniture, white embroidered bedspreads, a drift of muslin at the windows. Fat cream candles, a bowl of oranges and a few stone ornaments provide the decoration. Modern trappings – internet access, flat screen TVs – are all there but cunningly hidden. Dine in the barrel-vaulted dining room – crisp, cool, white – or under the gazebo. Sip cocktails or a midnight chaser by the pool with its glowing underwater lighting. Pretty magic.

Love time   Trulli quirky, trulli charming: take one of the alcoved trulli suites.
Love bites   Look forward to Puglian specialities with Med influences: octopus in pastry, courgettes tempura with cheese and mint.
Love it up   Spoil yourself Puglian style with an essential olive oil massage.

Bellissimo! ▶   Rustic chic in a trulli timewarp.

Il Melograno
Contrada Torricella 345
70043 Monopoli
T +39 080 690 9030
F +39 080 747 908
E melograno@melograno.com
W melograno.com
Roberta Guerra
31 rooms, 6 suites
Rates €300-450
Dinner from €220

Closed February

Extras  Courtesy of
Room for Romance:
Room upgrade if available
and a basket of fresh
fruit.

Airport Bari (65 km)
Brindisi (70 km)

Arrival From Bari: take the S16
for Brindisi, and at
Monopoli turn towards
Alberobello. After 300m
turn right following signs
for Il Melograno.

Il Melograno

Dazzling white 17th century houses grouped around a jasmine-scented piazzetta and fringed by olive groves give Il Melograno (the name means pomegranate) bags of Puglian charm. Five-star comforts make it one of the area's top addresses (Giorgio Armani, Mel Gibson and Goldie Hawn have all stayed) and its location, near the fishing port of Monopoli, can't be beaten. Owned by art collector Camillo Guerra and his family, the hotel is dotted with original artworks, antiques and old maps. Interiors are country-house meets Moorish, with kilims and white walls adding shades of the south to the classic floral docor. Spacious, inviting lounges are just the place to cool off in hot weather, while dining is al fresco and poolside. Virgin olive oil from the estate and freshly juiced oranges grace Il Melograno's famous poolside breakfast buffet, laden with pastries, flatbreads and fruit. The Guerras run the place with huge flair, and serenity rules: wander among the garden's pomegranate, fig and almond trees, and it's just you and the birdsong.

Love time   Lavish suites – some with two bathrooms – have intimate private patios.
Love bites   Dinners major on delicious local ingredients: artichoke and shrimp risotto, charcoal-grilled swordfish or loin of lamb crusted in Mediterranean herbs.
Love it up   Go for a pampering in the brand new spa, pedal off on a bike or take the hotel shuttle to the private beach at sister property La Peschiera.

Bellissimo! ➤   Classy country house, Puglian style.

La Peschiera
Contrada Losciale, Località Capitolo
70043 Monopoli
T/F +39 080 801 066
E info@peschierahotel.com
W peschierahotel.com
Giuseppe Guerra
8 rooms, 3 suites
Rates €470-950
Dinner from €180

Closed December – early April

Extras   Courtesy of
Room for Romance:
Fresh fruit and a
complimentary bottle
of wine in your room.

Airport   Brindisi (65 km)
Bari (70 km)

Arrival   From Bari: take exit signed
Monopoli Capitolo from
S16, towards Capitolo. At
the end of this road turn
right. The hotel is 800m
up this road.

La Peschiera

Practically lapped by the Adriatic's waves, La Peschiera is a magnet for hedonists who can't get enough of the beach life. What's more, this sister hotel to nearby Il Melograno is blissfully couples-only. The white single storey property – originally a 17th century fishery – has been artfully converted into an intimate little five-star hideaway where you can almost feel the sand between your toes. Any closer, in fact, and you'd be walking in the waves. Bamboo doors and tented beds draped in flimsiest muslin that feel straight out of the tropics lend a distinctly bohemian touch, while natural stone archways and simple white walls accented here and there with original artworks exemplify the hotel's understated style. This is a place to be as unsociable as you want: private sea-facing terraces with private sunbeds are set up for private dining à deux (no need to dress for dinner, then). Blissful indulgence continues with a fully-fledged spa and a menu of thalassic therapy and beauty treatments. The pool is softly lit by candle flares at dusk, but should you crave the bright lights, there's a terrific seafood restaurant here too.

Love time   Those close-up waves are a wanton invitation for midnight skinny dips.
Love bites   Seafood rules: scoff delicious fresh prawns, fried red mullet, grilled scampi.
Love it up   Hone your suntan on the private beach, book a full-body massage or dip in and out of the seawater, thalassotherapy and hydromassage pools.

Bellissimo!▶   Luxury seashore hideaway just made for two.

Borgo San Marco
Contrada San Angelo 33
72015 Fasano
T/F +39 0804 395 757
E info@borgosanmarco.it
W borgosanmarco.it
Alessandro Amati
14 rooms
Rates €150-170
Dinner from €60

Closed mid November – mid April

Extras

Courtesy of
Room for Romance:
A fruit basket in your
room and glass of dessert
wine after your meal.

Airport

Brindisi (45 km)
Bari (60 km)

Arrival

From Bari: take the
S16/E55 towards Brindisi.
When you reach Fasano
take the SS379 towards
Brindisi and hotel is
signed on the right.

Borgo San Marco

Turn off the main highway and you're deep in a southern landscape of 1,000 year old olive groves. Rising above it all is the blindingly white *masseria* of Borgo San Marco – a 15th century fortified citadel complete with watchtowers, domes and finials. Inside, it's all cool, rustic elegance with a dash of Moroccan exoticism – vaulted ceilings, stone floors, piles of cushions on low sofas, artful displays of pottery. Bedrooms – mostly two-room suites with private terraces – follow the less-is-more theme. Whitewashed walls, tiled floors and exposed stonework set off simple furnishings – rush-seat chairs, antique tables and iron four-posters – while linen curtains float at the windows. Courtyard rooms are more exotic – feast your eyes on soft Egyptian textiles, bohemian jewelled cushions and beaded curtains. Flop by the swimming pool on one of the teak loungers with a glass of iced lemon tea or don your shades and gaze at the glinting Adriatic, just two miles away, from the rooftop.

Love time   For a real hideaway, we'd pick the Del Vescovo suite with its own entrance and sea views.

Love bites   Chef Peppino uses many of his grandmother's recipes. We rated the eggplant parmesan and fresh oven-roasted sea bream with olives.

Love it up   You're not far from the Grotte di Castellana and fortified, medieval Ostuni.

Bellissimo! ❥   Check in, chill out and wave tensions goodbye.

Il Palmento
Contrada Cupa 161
70010 Locorotondo
T +39 0804 383 404
F +39 0804 383 397
E info@ilpalmento.com
W ilpalmento.com
Annamaria Montanaro
12 rooms
Rates €230-290
Dinner from €60

Open all year round

Extras

Courtesy of
Room for Romance:
A complimentary bottle of
wine and dried fruit, in
your room.

Airport

Brindisi (60 km)
Bari (40 km)

Arrival

From Bari: take the
S16/E55 towards Brindisi.
At Fasano take the S172
for Locorotondo, then
turn right to San Marco.
Hotel signed from there.

Il Palmento

This will stop you in your tracks: a village of tiny, meringue-topped houses that look rather like a forest of dazzling white beehives. These conical *trulli* houses, with their thick stone walls and pointed roofs, are unique to Puglia. We half expected to see a hobbit popping out of the room next door. More like little houses than conventional suites, the bedroom and bathroom are tucked either side of a central sitting area. Floors are tiled, walls are whitewashed, ceilings are domed while the furniture is simple and rustic. There are polished wooden dressers, rush-seat chairs, wrought-iron bedsteads and colourful checked sofas. Everything you need is here but done in a deliciously fuss-free style. Il Palmento's setting is equally bewitching; a sunny landscape of rolling vineyards and olive groves perfect for exploring the old trulli towns of Locorotondo and Alberobello. There's a cosy bar in the former wine press, an inviting pool and rose-filled grounds in which to wander. At night, you could be forgiven for thinking you'd stumbled into the Tolkienesque world of Lord of the Rings. And we could happily make a hobbit of coming back.

Love time	Cosy rooms are designed for intimacy. For added privacy, book the duplex with its semi-circular bed and rooftop terrace.
Love bites	Stunningly fresh Puglian cooking is served in the rustic-style restaurant.
Love it up	Play tennis or Italian bowls, or book a private massage and Turkish bath.

Bellissimo! ❧ Puglian living that's trulli special.

Masseria Il Frantoio
Strada Statale 16
72017 Ostuni
T/F +39 0831 330 276
E prenota@masseriailfrantoio.it
W masseriailfrantoio.it
Armando and Rosalba Balestrazzi
9 rooms
Rates €176-216
Dinner from €106

Open all year round

Extras

Courtesy of
Room for Romance:
A welcome drink on
arrival.

Airport

Brindisi (30 km)
Bari (80 km)

Arrival

From Bari: take the SS379
towards Brindisi, then
take exit marked Ostuni-
Pezze di Greco. Continue
on S16 towards Fasano.
The hotel is on this road
at km 874.

274

Masseria Il Frantoio

Turn off the cypress-tree lined road and into a landscape of ancient olive groves and poppy fields. Tucked at the end of a pine-scented drive is the bleached white masseria, or fortified farmhouse, Il Frantoio. But this is no ordinary farm. Surrounded by centuries old olive trees, a white-walled citrus garden and a wisteria-hung courtyard, this rambling 17th century building is a revelation in exquisite food, elegant rooms and genuine hospitality. Rosalba (she does the cooking) and Armando (he runs the farm) will take the very best care of you. Inside, all is cool white walls, vaulted ceilings, flagged floors and handsome country antiques. The eight simple but gracious bedrooms are named after flowers or blossoms. Original tiled floors, high ceilings, thick walls and vast windows keep them cool in summer and cosy in winter. There are soft lights and hand-embroidered linen, pretty wrought-iron bedheads and carved wardrobes. Before dinner, stroll through the garden, lit by tiny candle lamps, before surrendering to Rosalba's delicious cooking.

Love time	Turn up the heat in a bedroom with a real fire or cast-iron stove. The Room of the Newlyweds has a blissfully large antique bath.
Love bites	Dine under the stars off antique silver, old glassware and lacy cloths.
Love it up	Pack a picnic and head for the beach, or let Armando take you for a spin in one of his vintage cars to medieval Ostuni and Alberobello.

Bellissimo! ▶ Food for lovers in a timeless landscape.

Palazzo Baldi
Corte Baldi 2
73013 Galatina, Lecce
T +39 0836 568 345
F +39 0836 564 835
E hbaldi@tin.it
W hotelpalazzobaldi.com
Rosalba Meli
17 rooms
Rates €120-200
Dinner from €70

Open all year round

Extras

Courtesy of
Room for Romance:
A 10% discount on
the hotel's room
rates.

Airport

Brindisi (35 km)
Bari (145 km)

Arrival

From Brindisi: join the
S613 to Lecce, then take
the S476 to Galatina and
head for town centre. The
hotel is immediately
behind the Duomo.

Palazzo Baldi

Now this is grand living; not one 16th century palazzo but four. Tucked behind the cathedral in Galatina, in the heart of the Salentine peninsula, these small but perfectly formed palazzi were once home to local aristocracy. Step inside from the busy street, and a tangible calm engulfs you. Drift through high vaulted, marble floored rooms and you're back in a time of gracious living – a group of elegant chairs here, a grand piano there, with flamboyant artworks on the walls. The bedrooms are large, dramatic spaces elegantly furnished with a certain theatricality. Ceilings are dizzyingly high, beds richly draped; there might be a rococo mirror or a hand painted bedhead. Some have balconies, others overlook the inner courtyard, while the *nido d'amore* (love nest) under the eaves is true to its name. If you can drag yourselves away, Galatina is a great base for exploring this unspoilt part of Puglia. Return to your private palazzo and sip a cool drink in the leafy courtyard, or soak up the rays on the rooftop terrace – a secret suntrap.

Love time   These dramatically elegant chambers are definite breakfast-in-bed rooms.
Love bites   Rich red glassware, white napery, soft candlelight and zesty traditional cooking – this is dining you'll want to dress up for.
Love it up   Wander around lovely Lecce, with its rich baroque architecture, admire the frescoes in Galatina's Santa Caterina cathedral or head for the beaches.

Bellissimo! Grand living on an intimate scale.

SICILY & THE AEOLIAN ISLES

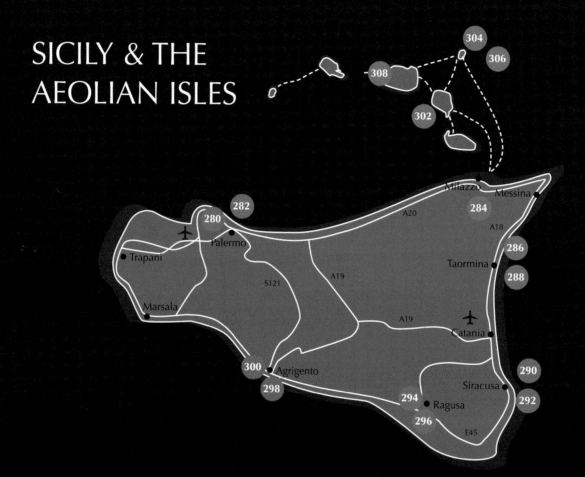

LOVE IT Sicily is the new Tuscany, in case you didn't know. And the Aeolian Islands – Lipari, Vulcano, Salina, Panarea, Stromboli, Filicundi and Alicundi – are incredibly chic. **When to go** Don't wait till the summer crowds descend – come and smell the almond blossom as early as February, guzzle fresh Sicilian strawberries at Easter or swim in warm island waters as late as November. **Don't miss** Snow-dusted Mount Etna – Europe's most unpredictable volcano; clip-clopping through Palermo's old town in a horse and buggy; Monreale's impressive cathedral; the mountain drive from Taormina to Terme Vigliatore; the "bikini girl" Roman mosaics at Piazza Armerina; Ragusa's old town – a masterpiece of medieval Baroque; the thrilling night-time ascent of Stromboli's island volcano. **Dine on** Spaghetti with capers and fresh tomato, fresh-caught swordfish, and arancine – fried rice balls filled with meat or cheese. Finish off with local cassata icecream, bursting with candied fruit. **Drink up** The local amber nectar – sweet Marsala or moscato dessert wine. In the Aeolian Islands, ask for vino Malvasia.

ISLANDS IN THE SUN

Pages 280-309

Centrale Palace Hotel
Corso Vittorio Emanuele 327
90134 Palermo
T +39 091 336 666
F +39 091 334 881
E centrale@angalahotels.it
W centralepalacehotel.it
Pietro Cascino
88 rooms, 15 suites
Rates €180-264; €208-319
Dinner from €58

Open all year

Extras

Courtesy of
Room for Romance:
A complimentary chilled
bottle of champagne in
your room.

Airport

Palermo (35 km)

Arrival

Take a cab rather than
drive into Palermo unless
you are steely-nerved.
Friendly front desk staff
will be happy to arrange
airport transfers. Valet
parking.

Centrale Palace

This haven of civility in the heart of Palermo – the perfect foil to the hurly burly of the streets – has a truly palatial feel. Gilded pillars and mirrors, tall columns and marble tiled corridors so highly polished you could skate down them lend the grandest air. Rooms range from the classically modern to the classically classic. Newer boudoirs have clean and simple lines, modern spotlights, black leather bedsteads and great bathrooms with modern mosaics. Older style rooms – some of which have a delightfully secluded terrace with wooden garden chairs – have Italian louvred shutters, muted tones and early 19th century furnishings. But the pièce de résistance here is the hotel's rooftop Ai Tetti restaurant – a stunning setting for al fresco dining on a summer's night. You'd be hard pushed to find a more alluring spot to take in the surrounding vista of domes, spires and rooftops – just the place, we reckoned, to fall under the spell of this beguiling city.

Love time	Canoodle over a bottle of prosecco on the roof on balmy summer evenings.
Love bites	Dinner (unless it's al fresco) is served in the peachy candlelit surrounds of the Ai Tetti restaurant, where you'll want to dress the part. Breakfast is taken in the impossibly grand 1892, with its soaring columns.
Love it up	Take a pony and trap around the city centre, or stroll through narrow backstreets, where market stalls jostle with exquisite churches and piazzas.
	A taste of the high life in old Palermo.

Hotel Letizia
Via dei Bottai 30
90133 Palermo
T +39 091 589 110
F +39 091 589 110
E booking@hotelletizia.com
W hotelletizia.com
Letizia Rusignuolo
13 rooms
Rates €115-150
Dinner from €70

Open all year round

Extras Courtesy of Room for Romance: A bottle of prosecco and a 10% discount in November and February.

Airport Palermo (35 km)

Arrival From Palermo central station: go down Corso Vittorio Emanuele towards the port. Via dei Bottai and the hotel are on the right near the Marina Square.

Hotel Letizia

Palermo crackles with life. Narrow helter-skelter streets crammed with age-worn buildings give way to squares and piazzas filled with grand mansions, palazzi and cathedrals. The Letizia is in just the spot for couples keen to stay close to the city's heartbeat (listen out for the church bells) without spending handsomely. Nearby is bustling Corso Vittorio Emanuele (posh shops) and Piazza Marina, considered one of the city's most romantic spots and minutes from its key cultural sights. Simple and characterful elegance is the Letizia's hallmark, and restfulness is the message. Reception areas are furnished with attractive mahogany antiques, gilt mirrors and Persian rugs. There's a lobby lounge and bar overlooking a small sun-drenched courtyard (great for sunny start-the-day cappuccinos) whose whitewashed walls have been livened up with arty murals. Airy bedrooms have antique wooden headboards, free-standing wardrobes, polished wood floors and (in some) jacuzzi baths for two. Staff are engaging and helpful; they'll be happy to tell you where to eat, people-watch and bar hop after the sun goes down.

Love time	Bedrooms – some with balconies – have an intimate and nostalgic feel.
Love bites	The hotel can arrange candlelit Sicilian dinners out in the evening.
Love it up	Trawl old Palermo in a horse-drawn carriage; go cultural; get spendy (Corso Vittorio Emanuele); swim n' sail (Mondello beach).

Pretty spot close to Palermo's pulse.

Green Manors
Borgo Porticato
98053 Castroreale
T +39 090 974 6515 / 338 434 0917
F +39 090 974 6507
E info@greenmanors.it
W greenmanors.it
Jannelli Verzera family
8 rooms
Rates €100-240
Dinner from €60

Open all year round

Extras Courtesy of
Room for Romance:
A room upgrade and
special in-room extras for
honeymooners.

Airport Catania (150 km)
Palermo (220 km)

Arrival From the A20-E90: exit at
Barcellona, then follow
SS113 towards Palermo
or Terme Vigliatore. Go
sharp left just before Terme
bridge; follow hotel signs.

Green Manors

Take the stunning mountain drive across the backbone of Sicily from Taormina to the north coast, and you're not far from Green Manors, an oasis of style and civility in the midst of rural Sicily. This old stone farmhouse has a wonderfully lush and secluded feel, and apart from the distant clip-clop of horses' hooves the only noise you're likely to hear is your beloved splashing around in the pool. Individually designed bedrooms glow with antique furniture, pretty objets d'art, expensive fabrics, fresh flowers and brass or wrought-iron bedsteads. Gleaming bathrooms come with embossed towels and sleek Etro toiletries. Old paintings and antiques give the dining room an appealingly rustic feel – log fires burn here in winter – while traditional, seasonal Sicilian dishes are given an innovative healthy twist. The garden is a riot of blooms in summer. Belgian owner Pierangela, who decided to give the place its English name, believes in doing the max for guests – she even came out and rescued us in her car when we got lost.

Love time	Be sure to book yourselves an Ayurvedic massage or pampering body treatment by the pool; all the lotions are specially prepared here.
Love bites	Don't miss Pierangela's summer picnics, complete with hampers, aperitifs and a barbecue. Indoors, try the Sicilian-reared pork, beef and game.
Love it up	Laze around the extravagantly big pool, and explore Sicily's northern coast.
Bellissimo!	Make yourselves at home, and you'll soon feel to the Manor born.

Hotel Monte Tauro
Via Madonna delle Grazie 3
98039 Taormina
T +39 0942 24402
F +39 0942 24403
E montetauro@angalahotels.it
W hotelmontetauro.it
Mario Mennella
85 rooms, 15 junior suites
Rates €200-283, junior suites €270-360
Dinner from €70

Closed mid Jan – late Feb

Extras   Courtesy of
Room for Romance:
A bottle of Sicilian wine
with nibbles.

Airport   Catania (50 km)

Arrival   Hotel is signed on
entering Taormina
village after leaving the
motorway. Access is
via a steep drive. Valet
parking on arrival.

Monte Tauro

This sleek, contemporary hotel perched on Taormina's cliff edge is a concerto in concrete. Clean lines, smooth surfaces and sweeping curved balconies spiralling down to the pool deck lend the Monte Tauro a futuristic air. Inside, polished wood, suede-effect walls, raffia chairs and shiny parquet floors are mixed with bold spot colours and outsize artworks. Needless to say, you won't find any frills and flounces here. Blond wood furniture, muted shades and full-length windows lend clutter-free rooms a restful air, while bathrooms revel in splashes of vivid turquoise and navy. The lobby is dotted with retro style '60s red armchairs, while a glass-walled lift whooshes guests down to the pool for some serious sunning. Sip a cocktail after dark in the piano bar, with its sculptured flowers and sleek black armchairs, or go for a stroll in the nearby Botanical Gardens at sundown, where kissing couples melt into the shadows. Torches illuminate the pool by night, mirroring lights strung along the bay. Whether it's the outdoor rock garden or flower baskets laden with blooms, concrete is turned into an art form here – and it works.

Love time	Your private decked balcony is just the place to entwine and soak up views stretching from the Gulf of Naxos to Mount Etna.
Love bites	We tucked into a great buffet breakfast and signature Sicilian cuisine.
Love it up	People-watch chic crowds in the bars lining Taormina's Corso Umberto.
Bellissimo!	Taormina that's far from trad.

Villa Ducale
Via Leonardo da Vinci 60
98039 Taormina
T +39 0942 28153
F +39 0942 28710
E info@villaducale.com
W villaducale.com
Andrea and Rosaria Quartucci
11 rooms, 6 suites
Rates €140-400

Extras Courtesy of
Room for Romance:
A complimentary chilled
bottle of sparkling wine in
your room.

Airport Catania (55 km)

Arrival Hotel is signed on
entering Taormina village
after leaving motorway
(otherwise follow signs
uphill for Castelmola).
Staff will park your car in
the courtyard.

Closed 10 January – 20 February

288

Villa Ducale

Perched right above cliffy Taormina, which tumbles vertiginously down into the blue Med, Villa Ducale boasts views to die for. To your right, Mount Etna's volcanic blue-grey cone smokes away, sending up plumes of white. Below you, the terracotta rooftops and purple bougainvillea of Sicily's top seaside resort cling to the hillside. We had trouble tearing ourselves away from the fabulous terrace, with its riot of yellow flowers (just the place for an early evening aperitif) and bird's eye view of yachts bobbing on the water way below. Bedrooms – all different and each with its own terrace – are beautifully styled with big mirrors, polished original tiled floors, wide beds, fresh flowers and immaculate bathrooms stocked with customised toiletries. Painted murals, hand-picked artworks and porcelain all add to the charm. There's also a sunny lounge, an old family library and incredibly helpful staff. Hospitable owners Andrea and Rosaria Quartucci are passionate about Sicily and delighted to share their knowledge with guests.

Love time   Every Mediterranean-style room has its own private terrace with sea views.
Love bites   Breakfast has to be the best in town: we couldn't resist the home-baked tortillas, veggie fritters and melt-in-the-mouth pastries.
Love it up   Take the hotel's free minibus shuttle down to town or to a private beach. Feeling idle? Soak in the hotel's outdoor jacuzzi on a shady terrace.

Barnstorming views from this ducal clifftop villa.

Hotel Gutkowski
Lungomare di Levante 26
96100 Syracuse
T +39 0931 465 861
F +39 0931 480 505
E info@guthotel.it
W guthotel.it
Paola Pretsch
25 rooms
Rates €100

Airport   Catania (40 km)

Arrival   From Catania: take the
A18/E45 to Syracuse.
Head for town centre and
follow signs to Ortygia,
the old historic district.
The Gutkowski is Ortygia's
only blue building.

Open all year round

Gutkowski

The only directions you need to look for are a couple of cheerfully peeling, powder blue and sand coloured buildings. Two former fishermen's houses overlooking the sea, they are the only blue buildings on Ortygia, the tiny, ancient island-heart of Syracuse. While their exterior captures the faded grandeur of the town – 2,700 years of Greek and Roman history – step inside to a breathtakingly pure and fresh modernism. This is not contrived minimalism but an unpretentious, unfussy, relaxed simplicity. Rooms are stark white, pared down to the essentials for a relaxed night's slumber – white bed linen, clean-lined contemporary furniture, unobtrusive modern lights and crisp, neat bathrooms. Glowing with natural light, there's clearly been huge attention here to detail. It won't take you long to wander around the hotel – a breakfast room, terrace, small reception and even tinier bar – but you'll want to linger in its intimate atmosphere. Staff are friendly and absurdly helpful. After absorbing the town's historic riches, tangled streets and seductive atmosphere, we found this the perfect chilled and relaxed retreat.

Love time	For some private sunning (or sinning), take the room with the roof terrace.
Love bites	Organic breakfasts include almond milk, home-made lemon and apple jam and home-baked cookies, eaten on scrubbed wooden tables.
Love it up	Stroll through Ortygia's narrow streets to Fonte Aretusa, the lovers' fountain.
Bellissimo!	Simplicity itself: white on white with splashes of blue.

Hotel Lady Lusya
Feudo Spinagallo 16
96100 Syracuse
T +39 0931 710 277
F +39 0931 710 274
E info@ladylusya.it
W ladylusya.it
Piero Truini
17 rooms
Rates €112-160
Dinner from €70

Closed 10 Jan – 28 Feb

Extras Courtesy of
Room for Romance:
A complimentary chilled
bottle of sparkling wine
in your room.

Airport Catania (40 km)

Arrival From Catania: take the
E45 and exit at Cassibile.
Turn right towards
Floridia. The hotel is 2 km
from here (signed), near
the Mediterraneo horse
racing track.

Lady Lusya

Named after the proprietor's daughter Lusya, this mellow old house painted in Mediterranean dusky pink sits pretty in acres of lemon groves. The villa itself oozes history – among the ancient exposed stonework, arches and nooks and crannies there are still shooting holes to ward off assailants with a revolver. The olive tree next to the pool – still producing healthy crops – is reckoned to be 2,500 years old, and you'll even see an original dovecote nested in the walls of the bar, along with the wine press and well of the original 17th century farmhouse. Owner Piero Truini and his wife have tirelessly restored the former rundown estate, even cleaning and re-laying all the tiles from the original terracotta floors. Puppies were gambolling on the lawn when we arrived, and the place is now a visual treat. The shady pergolas of the pool terrace beckoned for an afternoon siesta, and we were close enough to old Syracuse to go exploring later.

Love time	Our bedroom came with a high raftered ceiling, huge wrought-iron bed with gossamer drapes and enough room to throw a party.
Love bites	Guests have the option to order dinner each morning. We did, and thoroughly enjoyed our beef carpaccio and spaghetti alla vongole.
Love it up	Check out uncrowded beaches nearby where you can sunbathe off the rocks, and an original Greek amphitheatre performing classical plays.

This place lives and breathes the Med.

Locanda Don Serafino
Via XI Febbraio 15
97100 Ragusa
T +39 0932 220 065
F +39 0932 663 186
E info@locandadonserafino.it
W locandadonserafino.it
The La Rosa family
10 rooms
Rates €130-180
Dinner from €120

Extras Courtesy of
Room for Romance:
Room upgrade if possible
and 10% discount on
restaurant menus.

Airport Catania (65 km)

Arrival From Catania: take
the SS514 and exit at
Ragusa Ouest. Go to
town centre, look for Via
Mercato and after 50m
take Via XI Febbraio.
Hotel parking on the left.

Open all year round

Locanda Don Serafino

This small family-run locanda is nested in the depths of Baroque Ragusa, an incredibly well preserved hill town and now a World Heritage site. Converted from a 19th century mansion, it's designed to appeal to lovers of the good things in life. An arched doorway flanked by flowering terracotta pots welcomes you into chic interiors of honeyed stone walls, tiled floors, soft lighting and pale leather sofas splashed here and there with exotic oriental rugs. There are just ten pristine bedrooms – five of them suites – all furnished with handcrafted wood, subtle lighting from table lamps and simple stylistic touches. Rough-hewn stone walls and arched ceilings add impact and atmosphere. Fluffy bathrobes, slippers and internet access come as standard and there's even a choice of pillows to ensure you get a good night's kip. A short walk away, the labyrinthine Locanda Don Serafino restaurant is reckoned to be among southern Italy's gastronomic temples. Set in a tangle of narrow lanes, these atmospheric vaulted cellars were originally the stables of a 300-year-old palazzo and are stocked with over 700 different wine labels.

Love time   Get wet in the della Rocca suite, with its bathroom hewn into the rock.
Love bites   Make room for mouthwatering rabbit with bacon and pistachios, or a divine dessert made with Ragusano cheese and thyme honey on puff pastry.
Love it up   Historic Ragusa hides masterpieces of Sicilian Baroque ripe for exploration.

Baroque goes underground here, to chic effect.

Eremo della Giubiliana
SP25 per Marina di Ragusa
97100 Ragusa
T +39 0932 669 119
F +39 0932 669 129
E info@eremodellagiubiliana.it
W eremodellagiubiliana.it
Vincenza Jolanda Nifosi
9 rooms
Rates €120-360
Dinner from €80

Closed from 7 Jan – end Feb

Extras Courtesy of
Room for Romance:
A complimentary chilled
bottle of champagne in
your room.

Airport Ragusa (8 km)
Catania (80 km)

Arrival From Catania: leave the
Ragusa highway before
the town on the SP25,
signed Marina di Ragusa.
Turn right after 7.5 km
and follow signs for hotel.

296

Eremo della Giubiliana

With its own private airfield on the doorstep, this is a place to arrive in style. You'll love the Eremo – a 500-year-old former convent transformed into one of Sicily's top boutique hotels – just outside medieval Ragusa. Having annoyingly left the private jet behind we arrived in a no-nonsense Fiat, but couldn't have had a warmer welcome. Old beams and a palpable sense of history are everywhere. Enter the spacious lounge, with its ecclesiastical arches, huge stone fireplace and suits of armour, and you're stepping back in time. Guests sleep in the former cells, now artfully done out to pander to the most demanding modern softie. Pristine cotton bedding, wrought-iron bedsteads, beamed ceilings and antique painted armoires set the tone, while hand-milled soaps made on the estate exemplify the attention to detail. Downstairs, dine by flickering candlelight in the stone-walled vaults with their huge candelabra. Many of the ingredients are organically grown in the hotel's grounds, and the former farmhouse kitchens are now stocked with jams and olive oils to take home. Outside, lush walled gardens underline the feel of a forgotten hideaway.

Love time	Nuzzle up poolside on side-by-side chaise longues in dreamy gardens.
Love bites	Don't skip the delicious antipasti here: local grilled Ragusa cheese with honey, local foccacia and velvety zucchini served with black pasta.
Love it up	Head for the beach, stake out Ragusa or explore walking and bike trails.
Bellissimo!	Love and luxe go together here.

Baglio della Luna
Contrada Maddalusa SS640
92100 Agrigento
T +39 0922 511 061
F +39 0922 598 802
E info@bagliodellaluna.com
W bagliodellaluna.com
Ignazio Altieri
20 rooms
Rates €200
Dinner from €110

Open all year round

Extras

Courtesy of
Room for Romance:
A bottle of Italian
prosecco in your room.

Airport

Catania (185 km)
Palermo (190 km)

Arrival

From Palermo: take A29
and SS115 and continue
past Agrigento towards
Syracuse. Turn right
immediately after
underpass (3.5 km) and
right again. Hotel on right.

298

Baglio della Luna

Step through the gates here and you're in another world. You'll find this bijou little place on the edge of the busy city of Agrigento, just a mile from Sicily's famous valley of the temples. Baglio della Luna (the name means moonglow) hugs the prettiest courtyard, with flowers trailing from a profusion of pots, urns and baskets and rattan chairs perfect for basking in the sunshine. You could squirrel yourselves away in the 13th century stone watchtower, enlarged by Emperor Charles V in 1555 to repel the Saracens, where a shuttered suite almost straight out of Edwardian Kensington awaits with its own gallery floor, decked with antiques and an array of historic prints. The huge shady restaurant terrace of Il Déhors, the hotel's signature restaurant, looks directly across to the impressive 2,500-year-old pillars, columns and statues of Agrigento's Valle dei Templi. It's an excellent place to dine in the evening, when the temples are hauntingly illuminated. Il Déhors is also reckoned to be one of Sicily's top dining spots, and boasts an exceptional wine list. Another plus is the hotel's private beach just five minutes away.

Love time	We loved the deluxe rooms, with their pastel shades and pretty fabrics.
Love bites	Talented young chef Damiano Ferraro flexes his culinary muscles in the kitchen, putting his own stamp on traditional Sicilian recipes.
Love it up	Take a picnic and enjoy the 2,500 years of history spread out before you.

Touch of magic near the ancient city of temples.

Hotel Domus Aurea
Contrada Maddalusa SS640
92100 Agrigento
T +39 0922 511 500
F +39 0922 512 406
E info@hoteldomusaurea.it
W hoteldomusaurea.it
Ignazio Altieri
20 rooms
Rates €200
Dinner from €100

Open all year round

Extras

Courtesy of
Room for Romance:
A complimentary chilled
bottle of prosecco.

Airport

Catania (185 km)
Palermo (190 km)

Arrival

From Palermo: take the
A29, exit at Castelvetrano.
Take SS115 towards
Agrigento then Siracusa.
After 3.5 km turn right
after underpass, then first
right again to hotel.

Domus Aurea

If you'd sooner trade some old-world character for an extra helping of creature comforts, you'll be pleased to know that Baglio della Luna has a stablemate less than 400m away. Domus Aurea, its youthful sister hotel, has been created from an 18th century villa with Italianate wrought-iron balconies and other carefully restored features. Some period details remain, while furnishings are immaculate and shiny-new. Designed with comfort in mind, rooms are uniformly pleasing and smart, with lots of polished wood, well coordinated fabrics in rich reds and golds, and shiny bathrooms. Large windows overlook the mostly paved grounds, with their lofty palms, fountains, olive trees and urns of flowering plants. The best bedrooms look over the Agrigento countryside that inspired Pirandello and a line of other artists, as well as the Valley of the Temples. Splash out, and you can take one of the two superior rooms in the tower house whose terrace views span both ancient ruins and the North African straits. There's a well appointed lounge hung with oil paintings and plenty of places to enjoy eats and aperitifs al fresco.

Love time	Pick a room with a jacuzzi bath or make a beeline for the outdoor hot tub.
Love bites	Dine here or head up the hill to Baglio della Luna, whose first-rate chef has put his stamp on the region's gastronomy.
Love it up	Had your fill of history? Stretch out on the hotel's area of private beach.

Wealth of history outside; wealth of comforts within.

Villa Meligunis
Via Marte 7
98055 Lipari, Aeolian Islands
T +39 090 981 2426
F +39 090 988 0149
E info@villameligunis.it
W villameligunis.it
Manuela Tiraboschi
32 rooms
Rates €100-290
Dinner from €70

Open all year round

Extras

Courtesy of
Room for Romance:
Welcome cocktail on
arrival, room upgrade if
possible and free room
service breakfast.

Airport   Catania (100 km)

Arrival   Take a hydrofoil or ferry
from Milazzo, Palermo or
Naples. Call in advance,
and the hotel's car will
meet you on the
quayside.

Villa Meligunis

Lipari is the gateway to the Aeolian Islands. Bars and cafes spill into its buzzy little harbour, while chic shops line its winding cobbled streets. Beautifully reflecting the style of the town is Villa Meligunis, tucked away down a backstreet in the old fishermen's quarter, so narrow that even our taxi driver had to breathe in to reverse down it. While some of the building dates back to the 17th century, a newer wing has been seamlessly added 30 years ago. Inside, things are very much contemporary. Bold modern artworks accent the foyer and lounge, with its cool white walls and raftered ceiling. Rugs are scattered on tiled floors, while striking sienna coloured armchairs contrast with the creams and ivory. Upstairs, there's a dazzling rooftop bar and restaurant with Philippe Starck chairs and panoramic views over the town and the old walled citadel, floodlit at night. Menus use predominantly local ingredients, and our marinaded squid with baby celery and swordfish carpaccio was scrumptious. Manager Manuela is charm itself and – having lived in London for years – speaks flawless English.

Love time	Elegant bedrooms have a classic-contemporary feel with dark wood furniture, soothing shades and no stinting on quality.
Love bites	Tuck into hand-made pasta, harbour-fresh fish and delicious desserts.
Love it up	Take the hotel's shuttle to the beach, or rent a Vespa and head for the hills.
Bellissimo!	Stylish island villa where it's all happening up on the roof.

Hotel Quartara
Via San Pietro 15
98050 Panarea, Aeolian Islands
T +39 090 983 027
F +39 090 983 621
E info@quartarahotel.com
W quartarahotel.com
Maria Pia Cappelli
13 rooms
Rates €130-380
Dinner from €60

Closed November – end March

Extras Courtesy of
Room for Romance:
Champagne aperitif on
the terrace on day of
arrival.

Airport Catania (110 km)
Palermo (190 km)

Arrival Take a hydrofoil to
Panarea from Milazzo,
Palermo or Naples. (No
cars on the island). Call
hotel with your ETA and
a porter will meet you.

Hotel Quartara

This wonderful little find on the ultra-hip island of Panarea is the epitome of chill-out chic. Set back in a narrow lane, the Quartara is a magnet for well-heeled bohemians hankering after a taste of island life. A dazzlingly white sugar-cube villa with pillared whitewashed terraces, its seductive mix of oriental teak furniture, Latin American antiques and simple cool lines lend it a brilliantly original feel. Every room has a balcony – four having their own wide terrace and stunning sea views of the volcanic isle of Stromboli – with side-by-side sunloungers, tall terracotta urns trailing flowers and fat white candles to light at dusk. Antique Asian beds and four-posters are the centrepiece of uncluttered rooms, set off by moody lamps and ethnic splashes. Each has a different feel, be it colonial (our favourite), grand Chinese or minimalist. Kilims, lava stone floors, hand painted tiles and oriental art set off the lounge and dining areas, while the terrace bar, lulled by chill-out music and complete with hot tub, is just the place for a sundowner.

Love time	You're spoilt for choice here: will it be a champagne seduction on the terrace, in the bedroom or by the open-air hot tub?
Love bites	This is a place for intimate dining à deux. House specialities include fresh-landed grilled swordfish, carpaccio of prawns and pumpkin risotto.
Love it up	Hire a boat, pack a picnic (a bikini if you must) and spend a day at sea.
Bellissimo!	Island chic personified.

Hotel Raya
Via San Pietro
98050 Panarea
T +39 090 983 013
F +39 090 983 013
E info@hotelraya.it
W hotelraya.it
Miriam Beltrani
35 rooms
Rates €192-480
Dinner from €95

Airport   Catania (110 km)
Palermo (190 km)

Arrival   Hydrofoils serve Panarea
from Milazzo, Palermo
and Naples. (No cars on
the island). Call the hotel
with your ETA and a
porter will meet you on
the quayside.

Closed mid October – late March

Hotel Raya

This cult hotel on chic Panarea is the ultimate in bohemian island chic – just the place for lazily rich Robinson Crusoes to hang out. Lit by flares at dusk, the Raya's huge open rooftop bar draws a hip young crowd and is just the place to munch tapas and watch sparks flying up into the night sky from the volcanic isle of Stromboli just across the water (this is dining to dine out on). Everywhere here is made for outdoor living. Rough plastered walls in tropical white are brilliantly mixed with Balinese sofas and art (owner Miriam Beltrani lives in Bali most of the year). Rooms – some in a private enclave at the top of the hill – have cool floors and the simplest stylistic touches – a pot here, a wooden mandolin there, with wooden shutters opening on to a private terrace. Staff are charmingly laidback (don't expect Swiss efficiency), and after a day or two here, you'll be too. Amazingly, this little bit of island heaven boasts just two stars.

Love time	With silk gowns and flip flops waiting to be donned, a shady private terrace and a fridge stocked with bubbly, we couldn't tear ourselves away from our quarters.
Love bites	Dinner is served beneath the stars by mahogany-tanned young staff dressed (or undressed) in sarongs with bejewelled belly buttons.
Love it up	Swim straight off the rocks here, zip off in a speedboat or simply tan.
Bellissimo!	Hip hangout for island castaways.

Hotel Signum
Via Scalo 15
98050 Salina, Aeolian Islands
T +39 090 984 4222
F +39 090 984 4102
E salina@hotelsignum.it
W hotelsignum.it
Clara Rametta
30 rooms
Rates €110-280
Dinner from €80

Extras Courtesy of
Room for Romance:
A welcome glass of
Malvasia wine.

Airport Catania (110 km)

Arrival Take a hydrofoil from
Milazzo, Palermo or
Naples. Call in advance,
and the hotel will collect
you from the harbour.

Closed November – March

Hotel Signum

Greenest and highest of the Isole Eolie – the seven tiny Aeolian islands off the north Sicilian coast – Salina was the film location of Il Postino, that hymn to romantic longing. A clutch of ancient rural buildings in terracotta, ochre, warm yellows and pristine white make up the Signum. Vivid Mediterranean blues and sun-bleached whites are its hallmarks, while tumbling jasmine and bougainvillea add vibrant splashes of colour. What was once a derelict farming hamlet has been brought vividly to life, with shaded terraces and a maze of little paths meandering through the grounds. Various low-rise buildings house the bedrooms, where guests gaze out at lemon trees, vines (be sure to try the sweet Malvasia wine during your stay) and the bluest of seas. The Signum still has the feel of a little village (that's what we like about it); days and nights revolve around a generously shaped infinity pool with loungers, simply made for unwinding. There's candlelit dining on the terrace and fabulous views towards the neighbouring islands of Stromboli and Panarea.

Love time	Spread among houses in the gardens, rooms are simply furnished with wrought-iron beds, lace curtains and a smattering of antiques.
Love bites	Fresh fish and spaghetti in local caper sauce are Signum specialities.
Love it up	Spend hours by the pool, go picnicking, island-hop and explore wild untamed seascapes. Salina's clear waters are great for snorkelling.
Bellissimo!	This tiny island haven signals big pleasure.

WHAT'S ON AROUND ITALY

THERE'S NEVER A DULL MOMENT... HERE ARE JUST SOME OF THE YEAR'S MUST-SEES AND MUST-DO'S

JANUARY
Epiphany Fair at Piazza Navona
Rome
Celebration of the 12th night of Christmas.
Toy, sweet and present stalls, plus street
performers surround the Bernini fountains.

Roman Carnival
Pont-Saint-Martin, Valle d'Aosta
A host of toga-clad senators, guards and
nymphs celebrate with a real chariot race!
www.gransanbernardo.net

Ice Sculpture festival
Innichen, Trentino-Alto Adige
Contestants have three days to create
imaginative sculptures from 3m ice blocks.
+39 047 491 3149 www.innichen.it

FEBRUARY
Marathon of the Sea
Genoa, Liguria
Race held along the town's medieval streets.
+39 01 025 6182
www.maratonadelmare.org

Milan Fashion Week
Various locations across the city
The showcase of the fashion industry with
hundreds of shows for fashionistas by the

world's top designers.
+39 02 777 1081 www.cameramoda.it

Venice Carnival
Across the city
A magical orgy of balls, masks, music
and dancing.
www.carnivalofvenice.com

MARCH
Rome Marathon
Starts at the Piazza del Campidoglio.
Rome's traffic clears for the thousands of
runners who take to the streets.
+39 06 406 5064 www.maratonadiroma.it

Ravioli Festival
Casalfiumanese, Emilia-Romagna
Parcels of special pastries are thrown from
the town's ancient towers to onlookers.
+39 054 266 6223
www.comunedicasalfiumanese.it

APRIL
Maggio dei Monumenti
Naples
Private collections and buildings open to
the public, with special exhibitions.
+39 081 711 7580
www.maggiodeimonumenti.com

Scoppio del Carro
Florence
Easter Sunday
A pyramid of fireworks is released from a
cart in front of the Duomo.

MAY
Music at Piazza San Giovanni
Rome
Massive free music festival on 1 May
+39 068 069 2424 www.primomaggio.com

Teatro del Maggio Musicale Fiorentino
Florence
A season of opera, concerts and ballet.
+39 05 521 1158
www.maggiofiorentino.com

Eurochocolate
Perugia, Umbria
Calling all chocolate aficionados! This is
the place to scoff as much as you dare.
+39 075 502 5880
www.eurochocolate.com

Tennis Masters
Rome
Italian's grand slam tennis tournament.
+39 063 283 7200
www.telecomitaliamasters.it

World Festival on the Beach
Mondello, Sicily
Windsurfing, kite-surfing, beach volleyball
and all-night beach parties.
+39 0914 5348 www.albaria.com

JUNE

Rally del Salento
Lecce, Puglia
One of the oldest car rallies in Italy through
the Puglian countryside.
+39 083 231 4117 www.rallydelsalento.it

JUNE – AUGUST

Verona Opera Festival
Verona, Veneto
World-renowned opera season in the city's
2,000-year-old Roman amphitheatre.
+39 045 800 5151 www.arena.it

Festivale Musicale di Ravello
Ravello, Amalfi coast
Classical music concerts held in the
gardens of the Villa Rufolo.
+39 08 985 8149 www.ravelloarts.org

JULY

Il Palio di Siena
Siena, Tuscany
Teams compete by riding through the
streets in this famous horse race.
www.ilpaliodisiena.com

AUGUST

Time in Jazz
Berchidda, Sardinia
Top international jazz festival.
+39 07 970 3007 www.timeinjazz.it

The Venice Biennale and Film Festival
Giardini della Biennale and other venues
An international extravaganza of art,
architecture, theatre, music and dance,
plus the world-famous film festival.
+39 041 521 8711 www.labiennale.org

Rossini Opera Festival
Pesaro, Umbria
One for Rossini aficionados.
+39 0721 380 0294
www.rossinioperafestival.it

Ferrara Busker's Festival
Ferrara, Umbria
Parade of the best street musicians in the
world through the town's historic centre.
+39 053 224 9337
www.ferrarabuskers.com

SEPTEMBER

Couscous Festival
San Vito Lo Capo, Sicily
Gastronomic celebration of food from
Sicily and North Africa.
www.sanvitocouscous.com

Venice Historical Regatta
Grand Canal in Venice
The city's gondoliers compete in decorated
boats the first Sunday of every September.

Italian Grand Prix
Monza, Milan
Thrills and spills on the grand prix circuit.
www.italiangp.it

OCTOBER

Truffle Festival
Alba, Piedmont
A celebration of the famous *tartufo bianco*.
www.fieradeltartufo.org

NOVEMBER

Chestnut festival
Fanano, Emilia-Romagna
Eat up on the first Sunday of the month.

DECEMBER

Putignano Carnival
Putignano, Puglia
Floats, music and colourful costumes.
+39 080 491 1532
www.carnevalediputignano.com

Teatro alla Scala
Milan
Start of the big seven-month opera season.
www.teatroallascala.org

HOTELS BY TYPE

KNOW WHAT YOU'RE AFTER BUT NOT WHERE TO FIND IT? THESE LISTINGS SHOULD HELP

CLASSICALLY GRAND

Bauer Casa Nova, Venice
Centrale Palace Hotel, Palermo
Cipriani, Venice
Danieli, Venice
Grand Hotel Excelsior Vittoria, Sorrento
Grand Hotel Parker's, Naples
Hotel Caruso, Ravello

Hotel Hassler, Rome
Palazzo Belmonte, Salerno
Palazzo Niccolini al Duomo, Florence
Palazzo Sasso, Ravello
Relais La Suvera, Tuscany
San Clemente Palace, Venice
Splendido, Portofino

Villa Giustinian, Veneto
Villa Grazioli, near Rome
Villa Mangiacane, Tuscany
Villa Margherita, Venice
Villa Rizzi Albarea, Veneto
Villa San Michele, Florence

COOL AND CONTEMPORARY

Ca' Masieri, Veneto
Ca' Pisani, Venice
Cappello Rosso, Bologna
Capri Palace, Isle of Capri
Casa Howard, Rome / Florence

Charming House DD724, Venice
Gallery Hotel Art, Florence
Hotel Gutkowski, Sicily
Maison La Minervetta, Sorrento
Monte Tauro, Sicily

Novecento Art Hotel, Bologna
Savoy, Florence
Straf, Milan
Villa Meligunis, Aeolian Islands

BAGS OF HISTORY

Ca Maria Adele, Venice
Casa Verardo, Venice
Castello dell'Oscano, Umbria
Castello di Velona, Tuscany
Castello di Vicarello, Tuscany
Corona d'Oro, Bologna
Eremo della Giubiliana, Sicily
Grand Hotel Excelsior Vittoria, Sorrento
Grand Hotel Parker's, Naples
Danieli, Venice
Hotel Casci, Florence
Hotel de Russie, Rome
Hotel Santa Maria, Rome

L'Andana, Tuscany
Locanda Solomeo, Umbria
Loggiato dei Serviti, Tuscany
L'Olmo, Tuscany
Londra Palace, Venice
Metropole Hotel, Venice
Monteriggioni, Tuscany
Palazzo Magnani Feroni, Florence
Relais alla Corte del Sole, Umbria
Relais Il Canalicchio, Umbria
Relais La Suvera, Tuscany
Relais San Pietro in Polvano, Tuscany
Relais Santa Croce, Florence

Relais Torre Pratesi, Emilia-Romagna
Santa Maria Novella, Florence
Stella Maris, Liguria
Villa Abbazia, Veneto
Villa Giustinian, Veneto
Villa Grazioli, near Rome
Villa I Bossi, Tuscany
Villa La Massa, Florence
Villa Mangiacane, Tuscany
Villa Margherita, Venice
Villa Marsili, Tuscany
Villa Milani, Umbria
Villa Rizzi Albarea, Veneto

ON AN INTIMATE SCALE

Abate Masseria, Puglia
Albergo Milano, Lake Como
Baglio della Luna, Sicily
Borgo Paraelios, Lazio
Borgo San Marco, Puglia
Ca' La Somara, Sardinia
Casa Albertina, Positano
Casa Clelia, Italian Lakes
Casa Howard, Rome / Florence
Castello di Vicarello, Tuscany
Domus Laeta, Salerno
Green Manors, Sicily
Hotel du Lac, Lake Garda
Hotel Flora, Venice
Hotel Gutkowski, Sicily
Hotel Letizia, Palermo
Hotel Quartara, Aeolian islands
Hotel Santa Maria, Rome
Hotel Signum, Aeolian Islands

I Due Roccoli, Lake Iseo
Il Frantoio, Puglia
Il Palazzetto, Rome
Il Palmento, Puglia
La Fenice, Emilia-Romagna
La Magioca, Veneto
La Pergola, Lake Como
La Peschiera, Puglia
La Piana dei Castagni, Emilia-Romagna
Le Silve, Umbria
Locanda del Gallo, Umbria
Locanda dei Carugi, Liguria
Locanda Don Serafino, Sicily
Locanda Fiorita, Venice
Locanda San Verolo, Lake Garda
Locanda San Vigilio, Lake Garda
Locanda Solomeo, Umbria
L'Olmo, Tuscany
Masseria Serra dell'Isola, Puglia

Novecento, Venice
Oasi Olimpia Relais, near Sorrento
Pardini's Hermitage, Isle of Giglio
Relais alla Corte del Sole, Umbria
Relais San Bruno, Tuscany
Relais San Pietro in Polvano, Tuscany
Relais Torre Pratesi, Emilia-Romagna
Stella Maris, Liguria
Trattoria Gianni Franzi, Liguria
Villa Agnese, Tuscany
Villa Bellaria, Emilia-Romagna
Villa Clementina, Lake Bracciano
Villa I Bossi, Tuscany
Villa Mangiacane, Tuscany
Villa Milani, Umbria
Villa Poggiano, Tuscany
Villa Rizzi Albarea, Veneto
Villa Sanguigni, Lazio
Villa Simplicitas, Italian Lakes

HONEYMOON HIDEAWAYS

Albergo Milano, Lake Como
Ca' La Somara, Sardinia
Castello di Vicarello, Tuscany
Eremo della Giubiliana, Sicily
Green Manors, Sicily
Hotel Quartara, Aeolian Islands
Hotel Raya, Aeolian Islands
Hotel Signum, Aeolian Islands
L'Albereta, Italian Lakes
La Peschiera, Puglia

Le Sirenuse, Positano
Novecento, Venice
Pardini's Hermitage, Isle of Giglio
Metropole Hotel, Venice
Mezzatorre Resort & Spa, Isle of Ischia
Oasi Olimpia Relais, Sorrento
Palazzo Terranova, Umbria
Relais San Pietro in Polvano, Tuscany
Santa Caterina, Amalfi
Su Gologone, Sardinia

Villa Cimbrone, Ravello
Villa Ducale, Sicily
Villa Maria, Ravello
Villa Milani, Umbria

A REAL ORIGINAL
Abate Masseria, Puglia
Casa Howard, Rome / Florence
Castello dell'Oscano, Umbria
Costantinopoli 104, Naples

Hotel Locarno, Rome
Il Palmento, Puglia
Locanda del Gallo, Umbria
Metropole Hotel, Venice

Palazzo Baldi, Puglia
Relais La Suvera, Tuscany
Villa Abbazia, Veneto

BIG ON FOOD
Baglio della Luna, Sicily
Borghetto di Chiena, Tuscany
Ca' Masieri, Veneto
Capri Palace, Isle of Capri (Michelin*)
Eden Roc Suites, Positano
Grand Hotel Excelsior Vittoria, Sorrento
Hotel Bellevue, Valle d Aosta (Michelin*)
Hotel Hassler, Rome

I Due Roccoli, Lake Iseo
Il Melograno, Puglia
Il Palazzetto, Rome
L'Andana, Tuscany (Michelin*)
L'Albereta, Italian Lakes (Michelin*)
La Pergola, Lake Como
Le Silve, Umbria
Locanda Don Serafino, Sicily

Palazzo Terranova, Umbria
Palazzo Sasso, Ravello (Michelin*)
Rosa Alpina, Dolomites (Michelin*)
Tramonto d'Oro, Amalfi Coast
Trattoria Gianni Franzi, Liguria
Villa Margherita, Venice
Villa Maria, Ravello
Villa Meligunis, Aeolian Islands

SPA PAMPERING
Auberge de la Maison, Valle d'Aosta
L'Andana, Tuscany
Adler Thermae Spa, Tuscany
Borgo Paraelios, Lazio
Capri Palace, Isle of Capri
Castel Rundegg, Dolomites
Cipriani, Venice
Grand Hotel Parker's, Naples
Green Manors, Sicily
Hotel Bellevue, Valle d'Aosta

Hotel Caruso, Ravello
Hotel de Russie, Rome
Hotel Hassler, Rome
Il Melograno, Puglia
L'Albereta, Italian Lakes
La Peschiera, Puglia
Le Sirenuse, Positano
Mezzatorre Resort & Spa, Isle of Ischia
Palazzo Sasso, Ravello
Pardini's Hermitage, Isle of Giglio

Relais La Suvera, Tuscany
Rosa Alpina, Dolomites
San Clemente Palace, Venice
Santa Caterina, Amalfi
Schwarz Adler Turm, Dolomites
Su Gologone, Sardinia
Villa La Massa, Florence
Villa Poggiano, Tuscany

PEACHY VILLAS
Borghetto di Chiena, Tuscany
Borgo Paraelios, Lazio
Costantinopoli 104, Naples

Domus Aurea, Sicily
Gardenia al Lago, Lake Garda
Il Melograno, Puglia

Lady Lusya, Sicily
Villa Milani, Umbria
Villa San Pio, Rome

OUR OTHER EDITIONS

If ROOM FOR ROMANCE ITALY has inspired you to take off on a romantic getaway, you need copies of our other editions too.

ROOM FOR ROMANCE UK/IRELAND
is packed with details of 140 fabulous places to stay - from grand castles to intimate inns, in locations ranging from the Scottish Highlands to the West of Ireland. Whether your style is city sleek or rustic chic, moated manor or boutique townhouse, these are the places perfect for nights of bedded bliss. Price £11.95

"A gorgeous guide packed with romantic hideaways"
Daily Express

ROOM FOR ROMANCE FRANCE
is the consummate guide for a Gallic getaway. You'll find the creme de la creme of French hotels in this 164-page guide, whether you are looking for a sumptuous chateau in the Loire, a rustic Alpine hideaway, an intimate auberge in Provence or a chic townhouse on the Left Bank. Price £10.95

"Feeling frisky, passionate or head over heels in love? This guide checks out France's best beds"
Maison de la France Presse

OUT MAY 2006
ROOM FOR ROMANCE AUSTRALIA
Holidaying Down Under? This glossy new guide details great places to stay in locations ranging from beachfront and rainforest to desert outback. You'll find exotic island resorts, wine valley chateaus and chic boutique hotels in addition to homesteads and hillside lodges offering a real taste of outback Australia. Price £12.95

TO ORDER COPIES
You can purchase copies of all the Room for Romance guides by visiting www.room4romance.com and clicking on Buy the Book. Payments can be made online in pounds sterling, euros and US dollars.

Prices include all postage and packing (extra for non-UK residents) and your books are despatched within 24 hours. They can be attractively gift-wrapped on request.

FOR MAIL ORDER:
Call +44 (0) 20 7739 1434

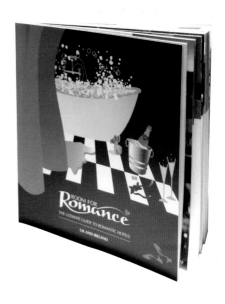

INDEX BY HOTEL NAME

INDEX BY PLACE NAME

COME SI DICE..? HERE'S HOW TO SAY IT

Could we have … ?	Potremmo avere ..? / Sarebbe possibile avere..?
A room with a view	Una camera con vista
A secluded / very private room	Una camera appartata
Your best suite	La vostra suite migliore
Bathrobes	Accappatoi
Bubble bath / special bath oils	Bagnoschiuma / speciali oli da bagno
Bathtub for two	Una vasca da bagno per due
A jacuzzi	Una vasca idromassaggio
Turkish / steam bath	Bagno turco (hammam) / bagno di vapore (steam bath)
Side-by-side spa treatments	Trattamenti spa (estetici/benessere…) privati in coppia
Kingsize bed	Letto matrimoniale 'king-size'
Canopied bed	Letto a baldacchino
Extra pillows	Cuscini supplementari
Red roses	Rose rosse
A bottle of champagne on ice	Una bottiglia di champagne in ghiaccio
Sparkling wine	Spumante, vino frizzante
Ice-bucket	Un secchiello del ghiaccio
A bowl of strawberries	Una coppa di fragole
Flowers and chocolates	Fiori e cioccolatini
Breakfast in bed	La (prima) colazione in camera
It's a special occasion	E' un'occasione speciale
We've just got engaged / married	Ci siamo appena fidanzati / sposati
It's our anniversary / honeymoon / wedding night	E' il nostro anniversario / viaggio di nozze / prima notte di nozze
Do you do special deals for honeymooners?	Esistono offerte speciali per coppie in viaggio di nozze?
Could you recommend a good restaurant nearby?	Mi può raccomandare un buon ristorante qui vicino?
Overnight room service	Servizio in camera durante la notte
No calls, please	Niente chiamate, per favore
Do not disturb	Non disturbare
Many thanks!	Grazie mille!

Riva Publishing Ltd, 4 Ravey Street, London EC2A 4XX T +44 (0) 20 7739 1434 F +44 (0) 20 7739 1424
www.rivapublishing.com info@rivapublishing.com